T0329277

THE INDICTMENT
OF
MARY QUEEN OF SCOTS

THE INDICTMENT
OF
MARY QUEEN OF SCOTS

AS DERIVED FROM A MANUSCRIPT IN THE
UNIVERSITY LIBRARY AT CAMBRIDGE,
HITHERTO UNPUBLISHED

WITH COMMENTS ON THE AUTHORSHIP
OF THE MANUSCRIPT AND ON ITS
CONNECTED DOCUMENTS

BY

Maj.-Gen. R. H. MAHON, C.B., C.S.I.

CAMBRIDGE
AT THE UNIVERSITY PRESS
1923

CAMBRIDGE
UNIVERSITY PRESS

University Printing House, Cambridge CB2 8BS, United Kingdom

Published in the United States of America by Cambridge University Press, New York

Cambridge University Press is part of the University of Cambridge.

It furthers the University's mission by disseminating knowledge in the pursuit of education, learning and research at the highest international levels of excellence.

www.cambridge.org
Information on this title: www.cambridge.org/9781107694248

© Cambridge University Press 1923

First published 1923
First paperback edition 2014

A catalogue record for this publication is available from the British Library

ISBN 978-1-107-69424-8 Paperback

PREFACE

THE MANUSCRIPT to which it is the principal purpose of this little volume to call attention is one of the treasures of the Cambridge University Library[1]. It has not hitherto been published. Yet it is of more than ordinary interest; in the first place because it goes far to set at rest the question of the origin and authorship of that final form of the Indictment of the Queen of Scots, which was produced at the Westminster Commission in December 1568, and known as the "Book of Articles"; and secondly because it seems to be a genuine example of the Vernacular Writings of George Buchanan.

It is not claimed that elucidation of this problem advances in a material degree our knowledge of the truth in that famous Cause, yet advantage arises in clearing up points on which Historians have been diverse in their views.

The Manuscript has been reproduced in accordance with the language of the original, except that the contraction marks have been reduced to a single symbol and capitals have been added to names of persons and places.

R. H. M.

February 1923.

[1] Press mark Dd. 3. 66.

CONTENTS

THE ARGUMENT

THE series of manuscripts in the Cambridge University Library, which have been referred to as the *Lennox Manuscripts*, was examined by Father Stevenson, S.J. and later by Father Pollen, S.J., neither has, unfortunately, published the result of his labour. Except Andrew Lang, no writer has used them. Lang had the advantage of seeing Father Pollen's notes, now lost, but the particular paper reproduced in this volume did not attract his interest and he passed it over with the slight notice, " In the *Lennox Papers* is a collection of ' Probable and Infallable Conjectouris,' an early form of Buchanan's Detection." The document is much more than this and deserves more careful attention.

The genesis and even the original language of the famous libel, known as the Detection, have been disputed. Ruddiman (1715) held that the Latin of the earliest known copy is. Buchanan's and in his purest style. Anderson (1727) believed the Scottish translation, which he printed in his Collections, to be Buchanan's rendering of his own Latin and he quotes a former Bishop of Rochester as to the ' beauty and elegance ' of the performance. Unfortunately for this view, we know now that the Scottish edition was not the first but merely a reprint in correct vernacular of an English edition which had nothing to do with Buchanan.

Camden in his *Annals* says that the Earl of Moray exhibited a copy, which must have been in manuscript, to Elizabeth's Commissioners at Westminster in December 1568 : " He produced Conjectural Acts (the Book of Articles no doubt)...*and* (my italics) Buchanan's Book entitled ' The Detection ' he delivered them to read, which found small credit etc... " Though Camden was probably mistaken as to its exhibition at this time, there is no reasonable doubt that the manuscript did then exist and was known both to Elizabeth and Cecil. Goodall (1754) says that he had seen a copy in manuscript which he believed to be the original shown to Elizabeth, but he does not say where he saw it[1].

Laing (1805) asserted that the *Book of Articles* and the *Detection* were one and the same, but Laing had not seen the MS of the former that now we know of. Hosack (1870) appears to have held the opinion that the libel was originally written in the Scottish dialect and others have followed him.

On one thing there is a consensus of presumption, amounting to practical certainty, that whenever it appeared and in whatever language, George Buchanan was the author. John Love, a critic of Ruddiman, strenuously upheld the *character* of his hero against Ruddiman's 'vile aspersion' that Buchanan had repented on his deathbed of his share in traducing his Queen. Love, in this particular, had the best of the argument. It had been better for that "*Lumen Boreale refulgens*" if his defender had been less successful!

It is by a study of these *Cambridge Papers*, and particularly of that now published, that we can arrive at a reasonably assured reconstruction of the course of events leading up to the writing of the *Book of Articles*. To simplify a subject that has been confused by such diversity of views as is expressed above I propose to treat it in sections, taking the successive stages from the emergence of the libel to its ultimate appearance as a printed book.

I. THE EMERGENCE OF THE LIBEL

Let us briefly recall the circumstances that gave birth to the libel. Mary had taken refuge in England after her disaster at Langside, on the 16th May 1568. The news of her flight

---

[1] This is an interesting problem. There is a manuscript in the British Museum (Cot. Cal. D. 1) which is probably a copy of the original paper. It refers to the Regent Moray as still living, 'Qui nunc prorex est,' instead of, as in the published versions, 'nunc et ipse occisus est.' But it cannot be the paper referred to by Goodall for it has appended to it another manuscript (Wilson's *Actio* referred to below) in the same hand, composed long after the Regent's assassination. Besides, although the Cottonian copy is damaged by fire it could not have contained the words on which Goodall lays stress, for the space is insufficient. (See *Examination of the Letters of Mary Queen of Scotts*, 1. 327.) In any case Goodall confuses Wilson's paper as a part of Buchanan's, which it certainly is not.

caused serious perturbation in the rebel camp. On the one hand Moray and his Party would feel confidence that once in the power of Cecil, the Queen would be securely held; on the other, Elizabeth's action was less easy to forecast. Her Majesty had a conscience, though it was of a kind that submitted to control. Moray had already had experience of it, and he knew well enough that it was necessary "to fortify his cause with sic evidente reasons as hir Maiestie may with *conscience* satisfie hirself"; the formula had been repeated more than once. He knew too that the presence of the Scottish Queen in England involved political problems of the gravest kind, internal as well as external, and that these would be weighed against the undoubted advantage of retaining her person with the consequent effect of lessening the danger of foreign influence in Scotland. Finally he knew that up to that time Elizabeth, to her credit, had refused to be a party to any scheme of a "speedy way to remedy the whole matter."

The first step was to provide Elizabeth with documentary matter sufficient, *prima facie*, to justify the retention of the fugitive and to withhold, temporarily, the fulfilment of her pledge of succour. She knew the story thoroughly already, she had expressed her disbelief in it, or in some part of it, but that was not the point at the moment; her conscience must have a tangible something, soothing and stimulating at once.

On May 21st (1568), that is within five days after Mary left Scotland, Mr John Wood was despatched to London. There is no copy of his instructions and the haste of his departure makes it unlikely that he carried with him any of the important papers which concern us. His duties are however known: "To resolve hir Majestie of ony thing sche standis doubtful unto." From the date of his arrival in London there was frequent communication with Edinburgh. On June 8th Elizabeth wrote requiring Moray to justify his proceedings; this letter sent by Middlemore arrived on the 14th, and on the 22nd Moray replied:

We have already sent unto our servand Mr Jhone Wode *that* (my italics) quhilk we traist sall sufficientlie resolve hir Majestie...We wald be Maist laith (loath) to enter in accusatioun of the Quene...sic leteris[1] as we haif...sufficientlie...preivis (proves) hir consenting to the murthure...Our servand Mr Jhone Wode hes the copies of the samin leteris translatit in our language...

The significance of these negotiations is too obvious to need comment. I suggest that it was at this date that the famous document, *afterwards* known as the *Detection*, first saw the light, and that it was in the form of a Latin summary of the case addressed to Elizabeth. To Buchanan, an indictment in the forensic style of the Forum would appear the proper preliminary to a demand for justice. The prosecution of a 'criminal' more highly placed and more guilty than Verres would appeal to his classic sense, and indeed, when we come to the *Book of Articles* and its five pleadings, there will be noted something reminiscent of the method of Cicero. In any case it seems obvious that some connected narrative would accompany the Letters, for several of them were, to say the least, obscure, and needed a gloss. The opening passage of the document is suggestive of Moray's expressed, but probably insincere, loathness to make accusation: "To us...quha ar dreuin to yis Streicht of Necessitie, yet quhais Faultis we desyre to couer, thair Liues we ar enforcit to accuse." So runs the Scottish edition[2], and the concluding words are equally suggestive: "Mony Thingis I haue omittit, and mony Thingis for Haist I haue bot lichtlie tuichit." *Haste* was clearly indicated, for not more than a fortnight elapsed between the departure of Wood and, *ex hypothesi*, the completion of the document; in that time a vast amount of detail had to be sifted and set out in a manner that would avoid inconvenience to others who might conceivably be involved should the affair not turn out as intended. To any other period to which the

[1] The 'Letters' referred to are, of course, the famous 'Casket Letters.'
[2] Properly this quotation should be in the Latin of the original, as the Scottish edition was not at this time made.

writing of *De Maria Scotorum Regina*[1] has been assigned it is difficult to see why 'haste' should have been necessary[2].

It has already been said that Camden is responsible for a statement that the first appearance of the *Detection* was at Westminster, when on the 6th of December the Earl of Moray exhibited various documents collected as evidence against the Queen, and several writers have followed his lead. But in fact there is very little doubt that Camden is not, in this, a reliable authority; no mention is made in the Journal of the Sessions at Westminster, nor in those of the Sessions at Hampton Court on the 14th and 15th of December, of the exhibition of the *Detection*. In fact in applying the title *Detection* to any document produced at these Sessions, Camden was in error, for this title did not come into existence until three years later. If by *Detection*, Camden intended to refer to the paper *De Maria etc.*, it is unlikely that *both* this and the *Book of Articles* would be simultaneously exhibited, for, as will shortly be suggested, the latter is but the final stage of what the former was the beginning.

That Buchanan was the author of the Latin indictment is hardly disputable; the date of the writing has been suggested above, and this will be more completely indicated as we go on. Whether he was also responsible for collecting the alleged 'facts' is a question one might wish to avoid; true or false, it should have been beneath the dignity of the author of the *Paraphrasis Psalmorum* to lend his pen to such degrading matter. The issue in *print*, whether of the Latin paper or of its translation, which occurred three years afterwards, was probably made without Buchanan's sanction or even his knowledge, and it is probable that he had this in mind when he wrote:

The over-officiousness of my friends, to precipitate the publication of what was yet unfit to see the light, and that excessive liberty which tran-

[1] The document was thus entitled in its first or Latin 'state,' the title *Detection* is of later date.

[2] A significant, I think unnoticed, item occurs in the Treasurer's Accounts of 1568; on the 27th May the Regent sent 'closed writings' to Buchanan, then at St Andrews. There can be little doubt that preparation of the *dossier* for Wood was the matter in hand and was complete before June 22nd.

scribers take to censure the works of other men, had altered many things and corrupted others according to their several humours[1].

Nevertheless the fact that he included a part of the Latin indictment in his *History*, is sufficient to stain his reputation with the same *atramentum sutorium* that, he tells us, 'cleansed' Bothwell[2], and at the same time to indicate him as the author of the original.

It seems likely that it was by way of a perfunctory apology to Buchanan, for the unauthorised publication of his paper, that a 'letter' often quoted, and most probably inspired by Cecil, was appended to the first printed issue of the *Detection* in the vernacular. It contained: "The book was written by him (Buchanan) not as of himself, nor in his name, but according to the instructions given him...by the Lords of the Privy Council in Scotland."

II. THE EARL OF LENNOX' CONNECTION WITH THE INDICTMENT

John Wood, emissary of the Earl of Moray, arrived in London towards the end of May 1568 to commence negotiations for the arraignment of Mary; the Earl of Lennox, then residing at Chiswick, would naturally be consulted and marked out for a leading rôle in the drama; as father to the murdered man and as legal pursuer in the Cause, it would be his part to lead the prosecution in what Moray and his party conceived would be a full dress Trial; the accused at the bar, the indictment, the evidence and all the rest of it. Cecil had evidently led Moray to this belief, for Moray's letter of June 22nd reflects the trend of the 'conversations': "We persave the *trial* quhilk the Quenis Majestie is myndit to have taken, is to be usit with

---

[1] These words occur in the Preface of the Latin *History*, but the date at which they were written is uncertain. It is at least known that the *History* had been in hand some time before 1577.

[2] It may be offered as some excuse for Buchanan, though not a good one, that much of the *History* was perhaps put together by an amanuensis after his infirmities had made him incapable of supervision. Thus only can the numerous contradictions between the 'official' story of Darnley's murder, which he put forward himself to the English Commissioners, and the version in the *History*, be accounted for.

grit ceremonye and solemniteis..." The foreign Ambassadors were to be present, the affair was to be public, it was to be hastened, "So as some good ende ensue before the 1st August." But this purpose was not maintained; a Commission was substituted, empowered to hear the statements on both sides while pronouncing no judgement. It cannot be alleged that this was due to reluctance on Mary's part to have her cause investigated, for she always desired it, provided that the presence of the Ambassadors was assured; in some degree they connoted the presence of her Peers, but more important they would ensure a faithful version of the result to their Masters and to the world at large.

From the first Lennox betrayed a desire to take part in the prosecution. Early in June Mary complained that Lady Lennox was urging him to prosecute her; and so we come to the *Cambridge Papers* which give us the results of his endeavours. There are four principal papers to be considered; three of them undoubtedly drawn up by Lennox, but the fourth, the most important of them all, is not attributable to him, but to—in all probability—Buchanan. It is this last that is printed at the end of this volume and with which we are chiefly concerned.

Of the *three* papers referred to, the first[1] is a narrative by Lennox, which contains a great deal that is very interesting, though a full consideration of it is not relevant to our subject. The MS is evidently incomplete, the first page and a part of the second are in Lennox' own handwriting, the remaining 10 pages are in a clerk's hand. It contains a weak, rambling story, overloaded with references to that 'Innocent Lamb' Darnley and his faithful devotion to his wife, much of which seems to betray a feminine touch. I think there is very little doubt that it is a rough draft of the 'Bill of Supplication' for an enquiry into the death of his son, or at least an enclosure thereof, sent by Lennox to Elizabeth; we know of this from the letter addressed by him to Cecil on August 18th (1568): "As I understand...the murder of the

[1] Cambridge press mark Oo. 7. 47/8.

late King...shall be tried in the beginning of September next; and as my wife and I exhibited a bill of supplication to her Majesty, as you know, requiring justice for that horrible deed...[1]." Whether the final copy was similar to the draft is impossible to say, but the value of our paper is that it represents Lennox' mind at a time when he was untutored by contact with the busy brains at Edinburgh.

One matter of outstanding interest in the paper is the quotation from a letter alleged to have been written by the Queen to Bothwell, from Glasgow, in January 1567. Andrew Lang in his *Mystery of Mary Stuart*[2] refers to this as the 'mysterious' or 'suppressed' letter, certainly nothing like it appears in the *Casket Letters* as finally revised. From a very full consideration of this, Lang derives the conclusion that the date of this Lennox paper must be subsequent to John Wood's arrival in London and suggests that Wood's copies of the *Casket Letters* contained the quotations referred to; for this and other reasons, Lang dates the Lennox paper as July. In this I think Lang is mistaken: whatever may have been the contents of Wood's copies of the letters, it seems certain that Lennox wrote before he had met Wood. His whole story is too much at variance with the official narrative put forward by Buchanan, which it must be assumed was the current Edinburgh version of the affair and known to Wood, to make it possible that Lennox and he were in collaboration at the time[3]. Thus the Lennox paper was probably written very

---

[1] P.R.O., *State Papers Scotland*, vol. I.

[2] Edition 1904, p. 175 *et seq.*

[3] It was Andrew Lang's strong point that Lennox quoted extracts which were practically similar to those quoted a year previously by the Spanish Ambassador from a letter which the Earl of Moray had told him about. And from this Lang deduces that Lennox must have *seen* the letter. I venture to think that two persons quoting independently at a long interval from the same letter would be unlikely to hit on the same excerpts, especially as the letter was a long one. Nevertheless the Lennox paper adds to the conviction that a letter did at one time exist which was afterwards suppressed, or alternatively that parts of the 'long' Glasgow letter were omitted. Malcolm Laing was ignorant of both series of quotations when he wrote, and Froude was ignorant of the Cambridge series. Perhaps they would have altered their views had they known of them!

shortly after Mary's arrival in England, at the end of May or early in June.

The remaining two papers can be taken together as the second and third Lennox narratives; a considerable part of the wording is the same in both. One is headed[1]: "*A brief discourse of the usage of umq^le the King of Scottis, sone to me the Earle of Lennox, be the Quene his wyff.*" The other[2]: "*A Remembrance after what sorte the late Kynge of Scottis Sonne to me the Earle of Lennoxe, was used by the Quene his wieffe.*" Both are of importance in tracing the course of events. The former is undoubtedly the earlier in date of composition, though neither is dated. Its opening lines: "Seing zour g(race) and Honours auctorized be the Q Maties Commission to hear and try the mater and that the L(ord) Regent of Scotland and utheris of the nobilitie and Counsalours thairof ar present...," show clearly enough that it was prepared for submission at York, to the Commission presided over by the Duke of Norfolk. It was written then during September or at latest in early October when the Commission assembled. Lennox was present at York though he was not at that time called upon to give evidence. Some of the phrases used indicate that the *Book of Articles* was even then in the making, or alternatively that the latter drew some of its matter from the Lennox paper. This will be referred to again.

As is pointed out by Lang, the extracts from the 'suppressed' letter, which were so noteworthy a part of the first narrative, are in this case omitted. Lennox has by now come in contact with up to date ideas! Buchanan, Wood, Maitland and Macgill were all present at York and they were the organising committee. Apart from the abandonment of the extracts referred to which implied a radical alteration of the original conception, there is evidence that the inner caucus had not even now completed the touching up of their measures. We must remember that what Lennox says *now* may be expected to square with what Buchanan and Co. had to say, for they

[1] Cambridge Press mark Dd. 3. 66.   [2] Cambridge Press mark Oo. 7. 47/11.

were working together. Thus we find that Lennox omits many of his first 'effects' which did not jump the right way and instead we have that the Queen :

Maks mentioun in hir lre sent to Boithuile from Glasgow...that he suld invent a mair secrete way be medicine to cutt him (Darnley) of(f). As alsua putts the said Boithuile in mynd of the hous in Ed^r devisit betwix thame for the King hir husbands distructioun. Termand (terming) their ungodly conspiracie *their affaire*.

Each of these three sentences finds an appropriate place, in practically similar words, in the *Book of Articles*, which we will refer to below ; but, though the first does occur in the letter from Glasgow, as we know it, it is very debateable if the second does, and it is certain that the third does not. For this and other reasons one must conclude that the letters as *privately* exhibited at York at the time this Lennox paper was written were not precisely similar to those put forward officially at Westminster two months later.

Regarding the third sentence, a curious point arises, which, though perhaps not strictly relevant, is worth a digression. The Bishop of Ross, Mary's representative at York, and of course in close touch with the proceedings, had evidently heard a good deal about the contents of the letters though it is pretty certain that he never read them. In his book, *The Defence of Queen Mary's Honour*, we find the following :

If ye (Mary's accusers) graunt us that ye were privie of the said letters... tel us, and blush not, how you could so readily and directly hit the interpretation of these words, *our affairs*...

In a later work (*De Rebus Gestis etc.*) he returns at length to the same topic, but in this case says that the letter contained a command that Bothwell should take charge of *her* (Mary's) affairs. Evidently whether the reference was 'our' or 'my,' it was a strong point much debated at the time, inasmuch as it involved the Queen in the act of Bothwell. But no such thing occurs in *any* of the letters as we know them !

We have, fortunately, the first few lines of the third letter, which was *not* sent from Glasgow, in the *original* French alleged to have been written by Mary[1]. It relates to, or is said to refer to, another scheme for killing Darnley: "Que je trouve la plus belle commodité pour excuser *vostre affaire.*" It is difficult to connect this with the reference to 'our affair' said to be in a letter sent from Glasgow, but in a Latin translation of the third letter, which will come before us again, we find 'nostra negotia,' and still more remarkable, the copy of the same letter at Cambridge has clearly 'our,' every other copy in Scottish or English or French has 'your' or 'vôtre.'

What are we to make out of this mix-up? The Glasgow letter does not contain what it is said to contain, and another letter is altered in the translation to exhibit something of the kind; it seems impossible to suggest a reasonable explanation, but at least one's confidence in the genuineness of the documents receives an additional shake! The opinion that at York things were still in a state of flux, is confirmed.

The third and last of the undoubted Lennox papers omits the reference to 'Zour Grace etc.,' it is apparently of later date when the Duke of Norfolk was no longer President of the Commission. It also omits the disputable matter mentioned above. There is now, as the only connection with the Letters, a suggestion that Lord Livingstone be:

Examined upon his othe of the wordes betwene the Quene his mistres and him, at Glasgow, mentioned in her own letter.

This third paper of Lennox' is, without doubt, that alluded to in the Journal of the Commission of the 29th November (1568):

The Erle of Lennox...cam to the said Commissioners and after lamentable declaration made of his natural grefe...and not being able to expresse his cause in convenient wordes, he put in wryting, brefely and rudely, some parte of such matter as he conceaved to be true...which wryting being conteined in three[2] sheets of paper...hereafter follows, *A discourse of the usage etc.*

The 'matter' in this document which Lennox 'conceaved to be true' does not concern us; he had collected a sheaf of 'fond' tales about the Queen, ranging from preposterous un-

---

[1] A complete copy, believed to be in the original French, is at Hatfield.

[2] The Cambridge copy is also in three sheets.

truth to highly coloured verity. Among the latter is the story of the quarrel between the Queen and Darnley at Stirling, on account of the numerous guard of Lennox-men gathered by Darnley; this is likely enough to be true and to have more bearing on subsequent events than is generally supposed. On the whole this last effort of Lennox is more cautious than its forerunners, he was apparently wearied of introducing statements which were unsuitable to a scheme that puzzled him by its intricacy. One gathers the impression that the English Commissioners were not greatly impressed by the taradiddles of Lennox, they wanted stronger stuff and they got it.

III. BUCHANAN'S INDICTMENT

Let us now take up the fourth[1] and most important of the *Cambridge Papers* under consideration, reproduced at the end of this volume.

Its full preamble is:

"*Ane informatioun of probable and infallable conjecteuris and presumptiounis quhairbie it apperis evidentlie y^t ye Quene, moder to our souerane Lord, no^t onlie ves previe of ye horrible and wnvorthe morthour perpetrat in ye persoun of ye King of guid memorie, his hienes fader, but als wes ye verray instrument, cheiff organe and causer of y^t Vnnaturall crueltie.*"

Lang's comment on this, that it is an early form of the *Detection*, is only indirectly true. It should be more truly described as an early form of the *Book of Articles*, but it has this close connection with the *Detection* that both are based, independently, on Buchanan's Latin paper *De Maria etc.*

The *Detection* in the Scottish dialect, or what is practically the same thing, its pseudo-Scots prototype, to be referred to later, is a close, almost literal rendering of the Latin, made in 1571 and done by an Englishman. *This* paper, on the other hand, is a free rendering of the *same* Latin, done by a Scotsman, and of a date *prior* to the exhibition of the *Book of Articles* in December 1568. The authorship is a question of considerable interest. It is perhaps too much to say that it is certainly by

[1] Cambridge press mark Dd. 3. 66.

Buchanan himself, but let us remember that from September onwards he was in London, actively engaged in preparing the matter required for the meetings of the Commission. The conclusion is almost unavoidable that to him would fall the task of interpreting his own Latin and setting it in a form suitable for presentation as an Indictment. The liberty taken with the Latin text, the occasional omission of superfluous phrases and here and there the correction of an imperfect original, all seem to point to the deduction that in this manuscript we have a genuine addition to the vernacular writings of George Buchanan, which Mr Hume-Brown might have included in his collection had he known of this Cambridge treasure.

In what follows I will distinguish this document as Buchanan's *Indictment* and in the extracts appended below compare his text with that of the Black Letter edition of the *Detection* of which there are two examples in the British Museum the language of which is the sham-Scots already mentioned. I may add here that in referring to the *Detection* I do not include the tract generally called the *Oration*, the two being always found together are often mistaken as parts of the same work.

The introductory passage of the *Detection* is absent in Buchanan's *Indictment*; this is natural, for it is merely apologetic, and apology was now unnecessary. But from this point onwards, item by item, the two translations are built of the same material, in the *same order* of setting, and with not infrequent use of the same phrase. The *Indictment* is usually the more concise, and in it a good deal that may be attributed to the admittedly hasty composition of the Latin paper *De Maria etc.* is rounded off or omitted. The following comparative passages taken at random will illustrate this:

BUCHANAN'S INDICTMENT[1]	DETECTION
	(from the 1st black letter edition[1])
To enter in ye declaratioun of hir *inconstancie towardis ye King hir huisband and how suddanele sche alterit hir affectioun after ye mariage*	*Begynnyng at the Quene's first inconstancie. For as in making of her mariage her lightnes was very hedlang & rash, so sodanely followed*

[1] Corresponding passages are italicised.

w^t hym or how fremitlie he wes wsit ye haill *vinter seasoun yairefter being sent in halking to Pebills, slenderlie accumpaneit,* restrainit fra acces to ye *counsele and fra knawleg of ye counsele effayris,* it neidis no^t now to be spokyn of sen nane y^t beheld ye proceydings in thai dayis ar ignorant of ye same. *That wes indeid ye begynnyng of evill* bot *thingis wes thane sa covertlie handallit* y^t naythar *ye multitude* nor zeit *thai y^t ver familiar* could compas or considder ye scope and end quhairvnto *hir intentioun wes bent.*

either inwart repentance, or at least outwart tokens of change of her affection without any causes appearing. For quhair before time the king was not onely neglected but also not honorably used, at length began open hatred to breake out against him, specially in that *winter quhen he went to Peble with small traine* euin too meane for the degree of a private man, *not being sent thether a hawking* but as commandit away into a corner far from *counsell and knawledge of publike affaires.* Nouther is it necessarie to put in writing those thinges, quhilk as thay were than as a spectacle noted of all mens eyes, sa now as a fresh image thay remane imprinted in all mens hartes. And *though this were the beginning of al the euills* that followed, yet at the *first the practices were secrit,* sa as not onely the *commoun pepill,* but alswa sic as *were right familiar* and present at the doing of many matters could not understand throughly, what *thing the Quene than cheefly intended.*

It would hardly be possible to select a passage which more fully exemplifies the opinion expressed above. There is conciseness in Buchanan's rendering, there is evidence of oneness of source, and there is the absence of ambiguity in Buchanan's translation of the sentence ' Non in aucupium,' etc. which a too slavish rendering causes in the other. For greater facility of reference and to enable the nakedness of the later translation to be judged, I have appended to this page the Latin of the original of this passage[1].

[1] The Latin text of the above passage from the copy in the British Museum (Press mark 600. b. 24) is as follows:

À prima Reginae inconstantia exorsi, vt enim praeceps fuit in nuptiis faciendis ejus levitas, repente ita sequuta (secuta) est vel poenitentia, vel (nullis extantibus causis) alienatae voluntatis indicia. Nam cum anteà non modò negligenter sed

Such comparative extracts could be multiplied many times, but space limits us to one more which I give for a special purpose.

INDICTMENT	DETECTION
	(from the same edition)

It is superflew to rehers ye haill circumstances of hir fremyt and vnnaturall dealing toward hym *ye tymes of ye hunting of Megetland and Glĕartnay*, bot evin as sche returnit fra ye last to Edinbur*, luggeine (lodging) first in maister Jhone Balfouris neir ye Abbay and then in ye Chekker hous, quhat wes hir behaveo* it neidis now (*sic*, probably 'not') to be keipit secreit being in ye mowthis of sa mony.

There went sche a Huntyng, *ones at the River of Magat, ane uther tyme at the forest of Glenartue.* There how coylye, yea how loftily and disdaynfully she behaued her selfe to the Kyng, quhat nede it be rehearsed, for the thing was openly done in all mens sight, & continueth emprintit in all mens memorie. Quhen sche was returned to Edenburgh sche tuke not her ladgyng in her owne palace, but in a priuate house next adioyning to Jhon Balfoures. Thense sche remoued into an uther house quhair the yerely courte quhilk they call the Exchequer was then kept.

This extract, besides confirming what I have said of the consecutive oneness of the matter, also serves to justify my reference to the first *published* translation of Buchanan's Latin as a 'pseudo-Scots' edition. There is something alien in the: "Once at the river of Megat, another time at the forest of Glenartue." The true Scottish translator puts it with a local knowledge that the other did not possess. *En passant* it may be noted that the mistake of 'Glenartue' for Glenartnay or Glenartna seems originally to have been a printer's error. The Latin manuscript in the British Museum (Calig. D. 1), which

parum honorificè Rex est habitus, tandem apertius odium erumpere coepit: illa praesertim hyeme, cum Peblium, non modo tenui, sed infra priuati hominis dignitate(m), comitatu, *non in aucupium missus est, sed procul à consilio*, et negotioru(m) publicorum conscientia, ablegatus. Neq(ue) literis committere necesse est, eas res, quae vt tum omnibus erant spectaculo, ita nunc, velut recens imago, in omniu(m) haere(n)t pectoribus. Et quanquàm hoc initium erat omnium, quae sequuta sunt, malorum, ab initio tamen occulta erant consilia: vt non modo vulgus, sed nè familiares quidem, et qui plurimis rebus gerendis intererant, satis intelligere, possent, quid potissimum tum Regina spectaret.

seems to be a copy of a document existing prior to the printed book, has the 'n' correctly, but all subsequent reprints and translations perpetuate the error which does not seem to have been noticed. It is interesting to note that, in this MS, while the Latin of the *Detection* has not been altered, there are cases in which the Latin of the accompanying *Actio* has been amended, perhaps by Wilson himself.

Let us for a moment recall the circumstances attending the issue of the sham-Scottish edition. In November 1571 Dr Thomas Wilson wrote to Cecil enclosing certain papers which he said he had, even then, translated into 'handsome Scotch.' From other evidence there is no reasonable doubt but that Wilson had been engaged in rendering the Latin paper *De Maria etc.* into what he was pleased to think was the Scottish dialect, and to this he had added a 'Scottish' translation of his own paper, *Actio Contra Mariam*, since known as the *Oration*. There was urgency in the matter, for Elizabeth had already authorised the issue of the printed Latin libel, it had been sent to the King of France and she was anxious to impute a Scottish origin to the whole affair.

From such considerations we are justified in concluding that the early black letter translation is the work of an Englishman, most probably Dr Wilson. A complete comparison of Wilson's translation with Buchanan's *Indictment* shows *consecutive* similarity of the incidents described, very much as in the case of the extracts chosen for examples above, proving, I think, that both papers, the one written in the autumn of 1568 and the other towards the end of 1571, are based on the same source and *that* the Latin *De Maria etc.* of Buchanan.

Further consideration of Buchanan's *Indictment* becomes so intimately connected with the document known as the *Book of Articles* that we will proceed to it at once.

IV. THE BOOK OF ARTICLES

Of this, the Official Record of the Session held at Westminster on the 6th December 1568 tells us:

For more satisfaction of the Quene's Majestie...they (Moray and his party) would shew unto her Majestie's Commissioners a collection made in writing, of the presumptions and circumstances, by which it should evidentlie appear, that as the Erle Bothwel was the chief murtherer of the King, so was the Quene a deviser and Maynteyner thereof; the which writing followeth thus: '*Articles contayning certaine conjectures etc.*'

Again on the 15th December the Record further describes the book:

...yesterday mention and report was made of a *Book of Articles*, being divided into five parts...

In 1870 Mr Hosack published for the first time a *Book of Articles*, divided into five parts, of which he had found a copy in the collection of MSS then belonging to the Earl of Hopetoun. This is now No. 33531 of the Addl. MSS in the British Museum. Hosack entertained no doubt that this is a genuine copy of the Paper presented by Moray to the Commission. In his preface he gives as his principal reason for this belief, the identity of the *Articles* "in various passages with the *Detection* of Buchanan, which was published some time after the Westminster Conference." And he adds:

It is clear, from a comparison of these passages, that *both* are not original; and as the Articles were in existence before the publication of the Detection the obvious inference is, that Buchanan inserted portions of them in his famous libel.

Had Hosack been aware of the Cambridge MSS he would have altered his views, though in any case it is remarkable that so able a critic should have formed the opinion that Buchanan composed the *Detection* by the simple means of extracting from the *Book of Articles*.

With the advantage of knowledge of the Cambridge Paper, which I have called Buchanan's *Indictment*, it is evident that Hosack was wrong. From what follows I hope to make it clear that the Hopetoun Paper, unearthed by him, is simply a rearrangement, with sundry additions and improved phraseology, of Buchanan's *Indictment*, the latter being related to the *Detection* only in that both are translations of the same Latin document done by different hands at different times.

Cecil had a passion for methodical analysis of the cases he dealt with; it appears in a hundred instances in the *State Papers*. He had drawn up with his own hand (29th June) a series of memoranda, *Contra Reginam Scotorum*, reminiscent of though not the same as the series now to be mentioned. The construction of the *Book of Articles* is suggestive of this habit of dividing the 'brief' into compartments; the eight *pièces de conviction* forming the documentary evidence of the *Casket Letters* had been arranged under headings, each being annotated with a brief indication of its part; thus: one to prove hatred and disdain, one to show the idea and practice of the murder, three to prove passion for Bothwell and three to prove connivance in the abduction and marriage. These four sections agree substantially with the first four chapters of the Hopetoun MS, the fifth chapter being devoted to subsequent events not referred to in the *Letters*.

It may be said with reasonable certainty that Buchanan was closely connected with the production of the Hopetoun Paper. The identicalness of the phrasing of many of its paragraphs with Buchanan's *Indictment* is too overwhelming to make any other explanation possible than that the *Indictment* was the basis on which the Hopetoun Paper was constructed.

Before giving some parallel extracts to exemplify this conclusion let us consider the title or preamble of the Hopetoun MS:

"*Articles contenying certane coniectouris, presumptionis, likliehoodis and circumstances, be the quhilkis it sall euidentlie appeare That as James sumtyme erle boithuile wes the cheif executour of the horrible and vnworthy murther perpetrat in the persoun of vmquhile king henry of gude memory, father to our said souerane lord, and the quenis lauchfull husband Sa wes she of the foirknawlege counsell devise persuader and commander of the said murther to be done and mantenar fortefear of the executoures thereof; diuidit in five partes.*"

The essential difference between this preamble and that quoted on page 12, of the Buchanan *Indictment*, is, that the latter involved the Queen only, *this* involves both the Queen and Bothwell. When Moray and his friends arrived in England their purpose was the prosecution of the Queen alone; Bothwell was a secondary consideration. The underlying idea of the 'suppressed' Glasgow Letter was that the Queen commanded and Bothwell obeyed, in the revised letter the reverse is the case; hence no doubt the English jurists found it necessary to include Bothwell as a party this being more in accordance with the evidence.

Now let us compare the matter in the two Papers; for greater convenience I have adopted modern English orthography.

BUCHANAN'S INDICTMENT

I

The King her husband hearing of her departing quickly followed by Stirling and came to Alloway, meaning to have attended on her according to the husbands duty to the wife. But at his coming there what cheer he received there, they that were present can tell. He had scarce (time) to repose himself, his servants and horses with meat, when it behoved him to depart.

II

...She spake in plain words to my Lord now Regent, the Earl of Huntly and the Secretary, and sore greeting and tormenting herself miserably, as if she would have fallen in the same sickness that she was in of before, said that without she were quit of the King, one mean or other, she would never have a good day in her life, and rather ere she failed therein would not set by to be the instrument of her own death.

THE HOPETOUN MS

I

Always the King her husband hearing of her sudden departing quickly followed, and by Stirling come to Alloway of purpose to attend upon her according to his duty. But at his coming he neither received good countenance nor hearty entertainment of her. And scarcely had reposed him and his servants and horses with meat when it behoved him to depart.

II

...She bursted forth in direct words to my Lord now Regent, the Earl of Huntly and the Secretary, sore greeting and tormenting herself miserably, as she would have fallen in her sickness and said, without she were quit of the King by one means or other she could never have a good day in her life, and rather ere she failed therein to be the instrument of her own death.

III

This unnatural dealing received of her in the sight and audience of divers foreign Prince's Ambassadors, so far directed him in courage that desperately he departed forth of Stirling towards Glasgow where his father was.

IV

...Upon the Saturday at afternoon she confronted them together, and never left to provoke the one against the other, till in her own presence she caused them from words offer straikes to other, and in her part it stood not but they had made an end of it there, for she was not careful who should be victor.

V

From the which returning to Craigmillar beside Edinburgh where she rested a while in the latter end of November, she renewed the same purpose, which she spoke of before at Kelso, in the audience of my Lord now regent, the Earls of Huntly, Argyll and the Secretary, proponing that the way to be quit of the king in appearance was best to move an action of divorce against him which might easily be brought to pass by reason of the consanguinity between them, the dispensation being abstracted.

VI

...It was a ruin unsuitable to have lodged a prince in, standing in a solitary place, at the outmost part of the town, separated from all company, a waste ruinous house wherein no man had dwelt seven years of before.

III

This her unnatural dealing in the sight and audience of foreign Prince's Ambassadors, so far directed him in courage that desperately he departed forth of Stirling to Glasgow where his father then made residence.

IV

...The same day at afternoon, and there confronting them never left to provoke them one against the other till in her own presence, from words she caused them offer straikes. And in her it stood not but they had made end of the matter even there, nothing caring who should be victor.

V

In the same month at her coming to Craigmillar where she reposed a while before passing to Stirling for the baptism, she renewed the same purpose which she spoke of before at Kelso, in the audience of the said Earl of Murray, now regent, the Earls of Huntly, Argyll and the Secretary, proponing that the best way to be quit of the King her husband was by divorce which might easily be brought to pass through the consanguinity standing between them, the dispensation being abstracted.

VI

...Which was unmeet in all respects for any honest man to lodge in, situated in a solitary place at the outmost part of the town, ruinous waste, and not inhabited by any of a long time.

VII	VII
This also is to be noted how her hatred to the King and his friends so continued after his death that she disponed his horses, armour and whatever else pertained him, to the very authors of his murder and others his greatest unfriends.	Also she disponed her late husband's horses, clothing, armour and whatever was his to Bothwell his chief murderer and others his known unfriends, in manifest proof of her continued hatred against his dead body.

I submit that the seven comparative extracts printed above prove conclusively that the document which I have called Buchanan's *Indictment* was before the writer of the Hopetoun MS. In the latter are quite a number of additional 'facts' not found in the *Indictment*, but of these the greater number are apparently derived from the information collected by Lennox, and I believe they are not to be found elsewhere. Thus, so far as the *matter* is concerned, there is I think no reasonable doubt that Buchanan and Lennox are the joint authors of the Hopetoun *Book of Articles*. Nevertheless I think it is very evident that some English mind supervised the putting together of the matter, and dictated much of the phrasing. It is clearer and more direct than the work of either taken separately, and much of the ponderous declamation of Buchanan is transmuted into the legal language of the day, though at the same time an evident endeavour has been made to maintain the Scottish character of the whole.

V. THE DATE OF THE WRITINGS

Turning now to the interesting question of the dates of the several writings, and whether the Hopetoun MS is likely to be, as Hosack believed, the final form of the famous *Indictment* presented as the *Book of Articles* to the English Commissioners on the 6th December 1568: if the reader will refer to the remarks made about the second of the three statements drawn up by Lennox, it will be seen that its opening words synchronise its birth approximately with the York Session of the Commission which commenced on the 4th October 1568.

The chief interest of fixing this date is the connection between this second Lennox paper and the Hopetoun MS. Items not to be found elsewhere are in both. The story of the use of a 'printing iron' to replace Darnley's signature on official documents, and the "word *fiat* in the place of his subscription," for example. The story that Darnley's body

> wes laid in ane pure (poor) hous...and yair efter lay twa dayis yair as said is yat al ye warld m^yt se him and thairefter caryit...to ye abbay w^t VIII or IX suddarts (soldiers)...borne vponn ane furme (form) and the feit vpwart and schot in ane hoill (hole)

occurs in the Memoranda[1] and is repeated in the Hopetoun thus:

> The Irascall people transportit him to a vile hous...quhair he remanit XLVIII houris as a gasing stok...she causit the same be brocht...be certane soldiours...vponn ane auld blok of forme or tre...(and) cast in the erth on the nycht...

Again both the Lennox and the Hopetoun relate in practically the same words that in her letters the Queen reminded Bothwell about the house in Edinburgh, also of the more secret way "be medicine to cutt him of (off)," and both have the reference to "our affairs" already mentioned.

Cecil's Journal, printed in Murdin's Collections, says that Moray and his party arrived in York on the 12th September[2]; Buchanan was certainly one of his company. It is hardly to be doubted that he would set to work at once to prepare his *Indictment* in the vernacular, based on his Latin summary. Lennox was at the same time writing his second paper; the pair must have been in communication.

It seems almost beyond doubt that the Hopetoun MS which drew so much of its matter from both was prepared at this time and was intended for submission to the Duke of Norfolk's Commission at York. Yet in fact neither the *Book of Articles* nor the Lennox paper was then submitted. Both were withheld until the following December when the Commission sat at Westminster. What was the reason?

---

[1] Cambridge press mark Oo. 7. 47/5.

[2] There is however an error in Cecil's Journal, Moray did not arrive at York until the 2nd October. Possibly Buchanan preceded him, Wood came down from Edinburgh and passed through York about that date, Lennox set out for York on the 24th and would arrive about the 26th.

A censor, whether Nicholas Bacon or another, was from the first supervising the legal aspects of the case and passing the various exhibits in review. Much that seemed promising evidence to Buchanan and Lennox was left out; the reference to Dalgleish and his evidence for instance; the Hiegate-Walker affair, which was probably a two-edged sword, and other things. Yet some details remained which did not tally with the evidence of the *Casket Letters* as we have them, nor with the general statements of witnesses whose depositions were to be produced; as, for example, that Darnley's body lay for 48 hours as a 'gasing stok' for the 'Irascall people.' The impression is given, almost the conviction, that in September-October the evidence was still fluid and in process of evolution. We have too that curious hint sent to Lennox by an unknown correspondent in Scotland : "But it is good that this matter be not ended until your honor may have the copy of the letter which I shall have at (shall send to) your Honor so soon as I may have a trusty bearer." This is undated, but likely enough it was the cause of Lennox dropping the extracts quoted in his first epistle, as we have seen.

For all these reasons it appears more than probable that the Hopetoun MS is not a true copy of the final *Book of Articles*, but that the latter was an emended edition of the former, bringing it into accord with the latest form of the evidence. This would account for the postponement of the appearance both of the *Book of Articles* and the third Lennox statement until the following December, when as we have seen the latter was purged of the doubtful references.

VI. THE PUBLICATION OF THE LIBEL

A word in conclusion as to the emergence in public of the *Detection*. During 1569 and far into 1570, negotiations were pending for the restoration of Mary's liberty. Perhaps on Elizabeth's part they were genuine, on Cecil's part they were certainly insincere. The barometer of foreign politics marked the rise and fall of Mary's hopes: in the summer and autumn of 1570 the glass was at 'set fair,' thereafter it fell and rose but little again. All the evidence, and there is a great deal of it, goes to show that up to this time the *Indictment* and the Letters had been kept secret.

Her correspondence was rigorously scrutinised, much that passed apparently unopened was read, deciphered, and added to Cecil's secret record. Before Bailey was arrested, or Ridolfi appeared on the scene, or Norfolk was examined, a great deal was known of her plans, and likely enough much was added to them about which she knew nothing. In March (1571) it was hinted that "her offences must be published." Yet Elizabeth still plumed herself on her forbearance in withholding the 'evidence' of her cousin's guilt from the world; and what is more to her credit, she resisted the importunities both of the 'King's Party' in Scotland and the Protestant Party in England to end all the trouble in a very summary way: "Never Prince hath had more warnings, nor better advice than she hath had to prevent all this long ago[1]."

By September 1571 the French King was becoming insistent on the fulfilment of the undertaking to set the Queen of Scots at liberty. To relieve this pressure every artifice was used to colour the examination of Norfolk with the maximum of matter damnatory to the captive; to add criminal to political guilt and so to move France to forego her championship, without jeopardising the treaty then pending, the publication of Buchanan's first (*Latin*) summary of the case was decided on. It issued, almost without doubt, from the press of John Day, a leading printer of London, and without any doubt it was published 'cum privilegio,' though there was no indication of date, authorship or printer on the title page. The intention was to impute to it a Scottish origin. I express the opinion that this edition of "Buchanan's Little Book" contained the Latin paper *De Maria Scotorum Regina* only, without any supplements, either of the *Actio*, Letters or Sonnets. No example of the pamphlet in this form is known to exist.

On November 1st (1571) Cecil sent a copy to Walsingham

---

[1] Leicester to Burghley, 4 Nov. 1572. Murdin.

in Paris, but the inference from his letter is that the Letters
did not form a part of the book; he promised soon to send an
edition in English with "Addition of many other supplements."
In the same month a copy was handed to Mary herself by one
Bateman; she described it as "Ung livre diffamatoire par ung
athée Buccanan." She does not so much as hint at the Letters
being included; it is surely inconceivable, had they been, that
she would have been silent.

On November 15th the French King, through Fénelon, expressed his "Regret that she (Elizabeth) should have permitted
such a villainous writing to be published." The Queen at once
denied responsibility; the books, she said, had been printed in
Scotland and Germany[1]; this was on December 10th or there-
abouts. In the meantime, and before December 5th, the book
appeared in the vernacular under the title *Ane Detectioun of
the duinges of Marie Quene of Scottes*, with the additional
information that it was printed from the Latin of 'G.B.,' that
is George Buchanan. To this work, Fénelon tells us some
"Rhymes in French had been added which are worse than all
the rest." It is impossible to suppose that this edition contained
the Letters; nothing could be *worse* than the 'long Glasgow'
letter, besides in all the examples which exist the Sonnets
(that is the 'rhymes') come first, and Fénelon could hardly
have omitted mention of the Letters had they also been included.

On December 10th, Fénelon, writing to his master, referred
to the approaching departure of Sir Thomas Smith for France,
"To conclude by alliance or by league a closer friendship with
France." In this letter it was mentioned that he (Smith) would
satisfy you (Charles IX) further in that affair (the remonstrance
about the libel). At the same time secret instructions were
given to Fénelon's secretary, who accompanied Smith, to relate
that the idea of the league was not seriously meant, but rather
that it was sought to obtain recognition by France of the young

---

[1] Germany was perhaps introduced to confuse the issue; some of the books in
defence of the Queen were said to have emanated from there.

King of Scotland and to an agreement to the perpetual retention in England of his mother.

Smith left England at the end of December. I have little doubt that it was then that the Letters (three of them only) were for the first time put into print (translated into Latin), and added, with Wilson's tract, "Actio contra Mariam," to "Buchanan's Little Book" already mentioned. The three letters were the *'clou'* intended to persuade the French King to concur in the desired policy. Apparently only a few copies were printed. A letter to Cecil, dated Jan. 10th, describes the distribution of three copies to assured persons. As the book was in Latin it would be of small service for general use and the publication of a French edition was arranged. This was published in February and Catherine de Médicis at once ordered its destruction. It is improbable that the Letters were published in England until after their effect on the French King had been tested, then they were grafted on to the existing copies of the issued libel in the sham-Scottish vernacular.

Fénélon enjoyed the reputation of being a warm supporter of Mary, at all events, poor soul, she trusted him as she had done so many others. But in this particular matter of the Libel it seems that he was more concerned with the successful accomplishment of the tripartite treaty that was to guard against the ambition of Spain, than in any question of a libel which his good sense would enable him to appraise at its true value. It is not likely that he was deceived by the 'Scottish origin,' but quite likely that he was prepared to accept it as such, and recommend it to his Most Christian Majesty as a means to satisfy his most unchristian conscience.

The date on which the final issue of the *Detection* with all its supplements, including of course the eight Casket Letters, took place is difficult to determine. We have the letter written by Alexander Hay to John Knox dated 14 December 1571 in which he states that the book had appeared in London. Hay does not say that he had seen it and he may have been making an intelligent anticipation of an event which he knew was about to take place; other considerations indicate a later date.

The remarkable thing is the ignorance of the persons who wrote in defence of the Queen, of the contents of the published volume. Whether it be the Bishop of Ross in his *Defence* or in his later *De Vita et Rebus etc.*, or Belforest in his *Innocence etc.*[1], or Adam Blackwood or any other, one feels inclined to suppose that they could never have seen the Letters as printed; what they allude to in their books are trifles compared to what they could apparently have objected. In some respects their ignorance is positive, as when they say that no one of the Letters is dated or has the name of place from which sent or the name of the bearer; the 'short' Glasgow letter has all these. Perhaps the explanation is that very few copies were circulated; Catherine de Médicis gave orders for the destruction of the French edition, and in England it is likely that only persons of known views had access to them. Yet even so it is surprising that those interested did not know more. Drury, the Marshal of Berwick, who was in the thick of the affair, had never seen the book even so late as June 1572[2]. Very likely he was not a solitary instance. It seems certain that from first to last Mary herself never saw the Letters.

In thus attempting to follow the course of these interesting papers I have refrained from expressing an opinion on the guilt or innocence of the Queen of Scots. The trial of her Cause was a travesty of justice; so much is certain, and the deductions made in the foregoing indicate to how great an extent Cecil manipulated the evidence. But even if we suppose all the evidence to have been false or garbled, we cannot therefrom claim to prove innocence. The true story of the 'Gunpowder-Plot' at Kirk o' Field has yet to be written; and when written, I believe it will be found to have little relation to the contents of Buchanan's famous Indictment or its connected documents.

---

[1] This work is said to have been compiled in England and sent to France to be turned into French and published.

[2] See *State Papers Scotland*, vol. II. under date 14 and 16 June 1572.

Summarised in a diagram the conclusions arrived at as to date of publication of the documents are as follows:

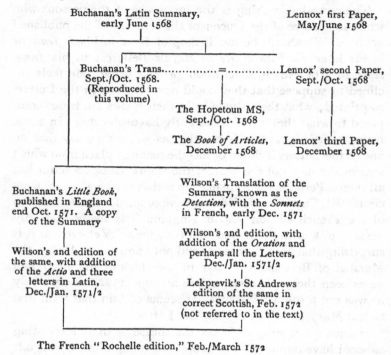

The French "Rochelle edition," Feb./March 1572

A word as to the *provenance* of the Cambridge MSS. Mr Jenkinson has kindly told me what is known: that they are possibly a part of a gift to the University by George I in 1715, and had been in the collection of John Moore, Bishop of Ely. The Bishop added to his collection by purchase at the sale of the library of John, Duke of Lauderdale, who died in 1682, but I can find no mention of these papers in the Catalogues of the auction, unless they come under the heading: 'A Collection of some things relating to the Kingdom of Scotland, MSS on Paper. Fol.' Although the papers may have come to Ely through Leslie, Bishop of Ross, who was confined there for a considerable time during 1571 to 1574, the more probable source is the

Lauderdale library. The Duke was grandson of John Maitland, brother of Mary's Secretary, the well-known William Maitland of Lethington. We have no record of what became of the Lethington papers, which must have been of great interest. It seems more than probable that they would come into the hands of his brother and so have passed to his descendant, and thence to their present home.

Lethington's claim to be the defender of the Queen while ostensibly acting against her is well known, and he would naturally have possessed himself of copies of as many of the documents passing at York and Westminster as possible. The Cambridge University Paper, now printed, is obviously a copy and done by an English scribe—perhaps surreptitiously for Lethington. It shows evidence of having been hastily transcribed, for there are many mistakes, and not a few instances where the copyist has overrun his lines and entered words out of their proper sequence. The errors have been preserved in the copy hereto attached.

BUCHANAN'S INDICTMENT

FROM THE COPY PRESERVED IN THE
CAMBRIDGE UNIVERSITY LIBRARY

Figures, thus (1) in the text, indicate the page of the manuscript.

The notes, which are numbered consecutively, are placed together at the end.

Capitals have been given to names of persons and places, and in some cases punctuation has been inserted to make the meaning more intelligible. Words which were deleted in the manuscript are placed in square brackets.

The general reader should have little difficulty in following the manuscript, remembering that v's, u's, and w's are used indifferently. Such words as wsit = used, vyif = wife, vn-vorthe = unworthy, neuer = never, look strange at first! The series, qlk = which, qll = until, quhen = when, etc. are more regular. In most other cases the spelling is more or less phonetic.

BUCHANAN'S INDICTMENT[1]

(1) Ane informatioun of probable and infallable cõiecteuris and presumptiounis quhairbie it apperis evidentlie y^t ye Quene, moder to our souerane Lord, no^t onlie ves previe of ye horrible and wnvorthe morthour p̃petrat in ye p̃soun of ye King of guid memorie his hienes fader, but als wes ye verray instrumẽt, cheiff organe and causer of y^t Vnnaturall crueltie.

To enter in ye declaratioun of hir inconstancie towardis ye King hir huisband and how suddanele sche alterit hir affectioun after ye mariage w^t hym or how fremitlie he wes wsit ye haill vinter seasoun yairefter being sent in halking to Pebills, slenderlie accumpaneit, restrainit fra acces to ye counsele and fra knawleg of ye counsele effayris, it neidis no^t now to be spokyn of sen nane y^t beheld ye proceydings in thai dayis ar ignorant of ye same. That wes indeid ye begynnyng of evill bot thingis wes thane sa covertlie handallit y^t naythar ye multitude nor zeit thai y^t ver familiar could compas or considder ye scope and end quhairvnto hir intentioun wes bent.

Q^w (how) in Aprill or yairby, 1566, returning fra Dumbar[2] to ye towne and fra y^t to ye castell of Edinbur^t (quhair sche cõtenewit till sche wes deliuerit of hir byrth) sche enterit (as veill apperis be ye successe) to compas and dewys ye wickyt and vnnaturall purpos y^t being ryd ane vay or vther of ye King hir laufull huisband sche my^t haif libertie to marie ye erll Bothuell, to bring ye mater to end and sche to be compted saikles of it sche begouth first craftelie in ye castell of Edinbur^t to mak ane dedlie hetrand (hatred) betuix ye King and ye Lordis qlk for ye tym attendit vpoun hir. Interteneing ye ane and ye vtheris in y^t consait as ilk ane haid soucht ye vrak (wreck) and lywes of vther omitting na thing y^t possibillie culd be practiset to caus yame yame (*sic*) enter in bluid, na thing thouchtfull quha suld prevail bot quhasaeuer lost thinkeng to gayn and ye mair suddanelie to atteine to ye p̃fectioun of hir

M.

3

intentit purpois. Quhat nobilmã at y^t tym presentit ye court bot ains wes put to ye strait to gansay as it wer y^t qlk he haid spokyn, or yane offer hym self reddie to defend his caus be armes or leif ye court. In speciell it is no^t to be past our (over) in silence[3] quhow ane ny^t amangis vtheris ye King abyding w^t hir qll (until) mydny^t wes past the summe of hir talk to hym wes y^t ye Lordis hes compassit his death and destructioun and immediatlie vpoun his dep̃ting sche send to my Lord now Regent, valknyt (awaking) hym out of his slepe and desyrit hym, all man^r of delay set ap̃t to repair to hir pñs (presence), quha according to hir comandmẽt past to hir chalmer sark alane onlie coverit w^t his ny^t gowne, at quhais cũing (coming) to hir presence ye substance and effect of hir haill harrang wes to hym, y^t the King hir huisband no^t onlie disdanit to sie hym in favo^r bot of determinat mynd purposit to tak his lyif at ye first occasioun. This wes temptatioun aneuche, bot God vald no^t suffer vicketnes [sa payntit] to haif sa payntit a clok nor yame y^t fearit hym to fall in sa dangerus a snar.

(2) Alwayis being deliuerit of hir birth, immediatlie ye erll Bothuell ẽterit in sic familiaritie w^t hir y^t nane bot he had aythar credyt or moyen to do ony thing at hir handis and first of all disdanand to haif other sycht or societie of the King hir huisband. Befoir ye [tym] dew tym y^t vomẽ (women) of basse degrie ar accustomet to remoif fra the hous after y^r byrths, sche past secretlie ane day in ye morning to ye New Havin and befoir ony knew, sche enterit in ane boit, cõductet be Ville Blacatter, Edmond Blacatter, Leonard Robertsoun, Thome Diksoun and thre fellows notorius pyratis awowit mẽ and dependaris of ye said erll Bothuell in quhais cumpany sche past to Alloway to ye greit admiratioun of all honest p̃sounis, that sche suld (have?) hazardit hir p̃soun amangis a sort of sic ruiffianis, to tak ye sea w^tout ony ane honest mã to associat hir. Quhat hir wsage wes in Alloway neidis no^t to be rehersit bot it may be veill sa said y^t it exceidit measo^r and all womanlie behaveour; the King hir huisband heiring of hir suddand dep̃ting quyklie followit be Streveling (Stirling) and come to Alloway, myndit to haif

attendit on hir according to ye huisbandis dewetie to ye wyif, bot as (at?) his cuming yair quhat chear he ressauit yair thai yᵗ wer p̄nt can tell, he haid scars (time?) to repois hym, his servandis and hors wythe meit quhane it behuiffit hym (to) dep̄t or do war, and sche cōtenewit yair four or fywe dayis yairefter na better occupeit nor of befoir.

It is sup̄flew to rehers ye haill circumstances of hir fremyt and vnnaturall dealing toward hym ye tymes of ye hunting of Megetland and Glẽartnay, bot evin as sche returnit fra ye last to Edinburᵗ, luggeine first in maister Jhone Balfouris neir ye Abbay and then in ye Chekker (Exchequer) hous, quhat wes hir behaveoʳ it neidis now (not?) to be keipit secreit being in ye mowthis of sa mony, ye erll Bothuell abusit hyr bodie at his plesꝝ, having passage in at ye bak dur fra maister Dauid Chalmeris hous yᵗ he wes ludget in, qlk wes nyxt wnto ye hous quhair sche remanit then. This hir self hes ofter yane anis confessit and in speciell to my Lord Regent and ye auld Ladie Louchlevin, wsand (using) onlie yis nakyt excuse yᵗ ye Ladie Reires gaif hym enteres quha becrasit⁴ hir, and he being enterit revisit hir aganis hir will, bot litill apperit of hir miscontentemẽt quhen as wᵗin few nyᵗˢ yairefter seing he keipit noᵗ his appoynted tyme sche send ye said Ladie Reres furth of ye said bak dur to bring hym, qlk Ladie fyndand ye dyk of ye zard difficill to pas our and sche being corpolent and vnhabell to clyme wes lattin downe in ane belt be ye Quene self and Margaret Carwod, qlk beltˢ brak and ye Ladie fell but alwayis sche executit ye cōmissioun⁶ sa quikle yᵗ sche causit hym arys frome his awne wyif. Nane yᵗ wer p̄nt is hable to deny this and ye maist p̄t hes alreddie confessit ye haill circumstance of ye same, lyk as wmqll (umquhile = the late) George Dalgleis ye said erlis cubiculair being in ye chalmer for ye tyme, confessit befoir his executioun to ye death yᵗ this haill arkele (article?) wes maist infallible and trew as his depositioun⁷ can testifie.

(3) At this tyme ye King remanit at Stirveling, in a maner exilit fra hir p̄ns seing quhan he wes p̄nt he nowther culd fynd favour nor Intertenement to hym and his servandis bot con-

tinuall slyting proceidit in tryfles and forget querrellis alwayis
he returnit to Edinbur^t and w^t all humilitie requyrit hir favour
and to be admitted to hir bed as hir huisband, qlk altogether
wes denyet, and sa in dispair wes constranit to pas agane to
ye vest cuntrie to drywe (drive) over his cairfull and miserable
tyme.

Sone heirefter conclusioun being takyn to pas to Jedbur^t for
halding of ane Justice Air in ye begynnyng of October 1566,
ye said erll maid ane reid (raid) in Lyddisdaill quhair, as is
veill knawin, he chancit of a theif to be hurt and woundit, sche,
ressauing ye aduertismet of it at Borthuik [ane] as ane rathar en-
ragit then in hir ry^t wyt, poistet fordwart to Melros and fra y^t to
Jedbur^t quhair na aduertismet of his being on lyf culd satisfye
hir bot vtterang hir Inordinat affectioun, sche hazard hir self
in ane sessoun of ye zeir maist vnganand (unsuitable) be a
passaige vncouth, strait and difficill and in ye cumpanye of
sic a cowoy (convoy) as na prewat ma of honest reputatioun
wald haif enterit amang^s, passand to ye Armetage (Hermitage)
in Lyddisdaill and returnand to Jedbur^t one ane schort wynter
day quhair sche preparit all thingis meit for his transporting,
and schortlie, being broucht y^r it wer vthervyis vsit be hyr nor
it becumyt hir to offer or hym to ressaue, yis faschius and ex-
traordinare trawaill vnd^s ny^t bot rathar in Goddis Jugement
put hir in sic extreme infirmitie as few luikyt for hir lyif, ye
knawlege quhairof cuing to ye eares of ye King hir huisband,
resident at Stirling he deleyit no^t bot w^t all speid come to
Jedburghe to veseit and confort hir. How he wes ressauit, thai
y^t wer pnt can best tell gif other he ressauit guid wordis or
guid countenance, gif other meit, drink or ludgeine wes preparit
or appoyntet for hym, bot ye haill Lordis and officieris of court
yair attending expreslie comandit y^t ane of yame suld ains
luik to hym or schaw hym favour, and fering y^t my Lord now
Regent suld schaw hym y^t benevolence to gif hym his chalm^r
for a ny^t my Lordis vyif wes spedelie sent to ye hous and
comandit to pas to hir bed and contrafeict hir self to be seik,
to ye end ye King suld no^t swyt (suit = beg for) ye ludgene

or in cais he soucht ye same y^t hir seiknes my^t be ane sufficient
excuse fra remaining yair onlie a ny^t, maist fremytlie inter-
teneit he returnit agane to his purgatorie na thing conforted
of his jornay[10]; bot quhen all yis difficultie wes maid to gar
(deny) hym ludgeine, meit and drink for a ny^t, the erll Bothuell
wes transported of befoir fra his comoune ludgeine and placit
in ye Quenis hous in ye chalmer derect vnder hir awne quhome
in hir gretest extremitie sche [sparest] sparit no^t to vesite, sche
wes seik in deid and he hurt bot befoir thai remowit furth of y^t
ludgeine itt wes planlie aneuche spokyn and no^t w^{t}out caus y^t
he abusit hir bodie as of befoir.

(4) About ye fyft day of November removing frome Jedburghe to Kelso yair come ane man of ye Kingis to ye Quene
wyth letteres, after ye reiding thairof sche spak in plane wordis
to my Lord now Regent, ye erll of Huntlie and ye Secretar
and sair gretand (weeping) and tormentand hir self miserabillie
as gif sche wald haif fallin in ye same seiknes y^t sche wes in of
befoir said y^t wy^{t}out sche wer quyt of ye King be ane meane
or wther sche culd never haif ane guid day in hir lyif and rathar
or sche faillit yairin wald no^t set by to be ye instrumẽt of hir
awne death[11].

At the same tyme in hir progres throwche ye Mers ye ny^t
sche restet at Coldinghame it is certane y^t ye Ladie Reires wes
tane gangand throuche ye watche and quha wes in cumpany
w^t hir or quhat wes ye purpois or occasioun of yair walking y^t
tyme of ny^t ye Quene hir self can tell.

Fra the qlk returning to Craigmillar besyd Edinbur^t quhair
sche restit ane quhill in ye end of Nouv̂ber sche renewit ye
same purpois qlk sche spak of befoir at Kelso, in ye audience
of my Lord now Regent, ye erll of Huntlie, Argyll and ye
Secretar proponyng y^t the way to be quyte of ye King, in
apperance wes best, to mowe ane actioun of diuorce aganis
hym qlk my^t aeselie be broucht to pas be reasoun of ye
cõsanguinitie betuix yame ye dispensatioun being abstractit[12],
quhairvnto it wes ansuerit how y^t culd no^t gudlie be done
w^{t}out hazard y^t be ye doing yairof ye King, now our souerane,

hir sonne suld be declarit bastard sene nathar he nor sche
cõtractit y^t mariage being ignorant of ye degreis of consanguinitie quhairin thai stuid; qlk ans^r quhan sche haid pansit[13]
vpoun sche left y^t consait and opinioun of ye deiuorce (divorce)
and euer frome y^t day furth imaginit and devisit how to cut
hym away as be ye sequele of yis discourse mair planlie sall
appeir.

The King cõing agane frome Stirveling to Craigmillar to
wesit hir thinkand hir passioun and coleir sumquhat mitigat,
he profeitit nathing nowther getting guid countenance, guid
traitmẽt nor permissioun to pas w^t hir to bed howbeit in all
yis tyme it wes suspectit no^t w^{t}out caus y^t the erll Bothuell
abusit hir bodie as of befoir.

At the begynning of December sche addressit to Stirling
becaus of ye embassatouris arrywit for ye baptisme of ye
King now our souerane, agane qlk sche preparit and gaif to
ye said erll Bothuell out of hir awne couferis, or cost be hir
money, diuers riche abulzeamẽtis at ye making quhairof hir
self wes maister of vark and tuik na les attendence y^t all
thingis meit for ye decoratioun y^{r}of wer had, nor gif sche
haid bene his servand. Howbeit on ye vther p̃t ye King hir
laufull huisband wes left desolat, na kynd of preparatioun maid
for y^t qlk my^t haif tendit for his hono^r or avancem̃t at sic a
tyme and no^t onlie ver ye embassato^{rs} inhibit to spek wy^t hym
or he p̃t (*sic*) p̃mitted to resort to y^r presence being all w^{t}in
Streveling Castell bot ye haill nobilmẽ and sum officiaris y^t be
hir awne appoyntment wer derectit of befoir to haif attendit
to (5) his seruice wer commandit no^t to accumpanye hym nor
samekill as anis to schaw hym gude countenance or do hym
courtesie.

This vnnaturall dealing ressauit of hir in ye sy^t and audience
of diuers foren princes embassadouris sa far derectit hym in
curage y^t disparetlie he dep̃tit furth of Stirveling towardis
Glescow quhair his father wes, at ye end of December. Gif he
ressauit ony thing befoir his dep̃ting y^t wes ye occasioun of his
strange an vncouth seiknes y^t suddanlie he fell in or quhether

his seiknes wes artificiell or naturall, God knawis, bot trew it is y^t befoir he rod a my^l out of Stirveling he felt ye begynnyng of y^t plaig qlk y^{r}efter sa inquietit hym; and it my^t wele be vnderstand quhat favo^r sche buir vnto hym, or rathar quhow bent sche wes to do hym disples^r and dishono^r quhan at his dep̄ting frome Stirling sche causit all ye plat and siluer weschell appoynted for hym and qlk he haid wset continuallie of befoir fra his mariage to be takin fra hym and tyn weschell (tin vessels) to be gevin in place y^{r}of.

Efter ye baptisme sche causit my Lord now Regent desyr ye erll Bothuell to ryd to Sanctandr̃s (St Andrews) quhen my Lord of Bedfurd ye Quenis maiesteis of Englandis embassadour for ye tyme past to ther, quha promisit sa to do, howbeit nathing wes les in his mynd or in ye mynd of hir y^t sua devisit, that, howsonne y^t euer thai wer dep̄tet to Sanctandr̃s and ye King to Glescow, sche w^t ye erll Bothuele past to Drymen^{14}; in quhat ordo^r sche and he wes chalmerit y^r anew (enough) saw, y^t lykit litill ye man^r, baithe the houses sa cōvenit y^t he resorted and lay w^t hir at his ples^r and lykwys at Tullibardin, in qlk tua houss sche abaid ye spece of aucht dayis vsand y^t fylthines almoist w^{t}out cloik or respect of schame or honestie.

Returning agane to Stirveling at ye begynnyng of Januar sche begouth to fynd fault w^t the house quhair ye King hir sonne wes nurisset (nursed) as that it wes evill ayrit and wald be ye occasioun of rewmes (rheum) and cattaris althoucht na sic thing apperit or haid ony schaw of probabilitie, it being in the myddis of vynter and in cais it haid bene symmer, that hous is alswell situat and als cōvenient to dwell in for respect of ye air and vthervayis, as ony vther hous in Scotland; bot that wes no^t the scope or force, he behuiffyt to be careit in ye cauld vynter to Edinbur^t, quhair schortlie sche tuik purpois to execut y^t malice qlk sche haid lang borne in hir hart; and sua preparit hir self fra Edindughe (*sic*) to ryd to Glescow in ye end of Januar to veseit the King hir huisband y^t almaist be ye space of ane monith haid cōtenewit yair in seiknes vncowth and mervelous to behauld, of mynd as veill apperis be hir Letteris, to bring hym to [his] Edinbur^t to his fatall end and finall destructioun, qlk sche vald neuer attempt no^t having hir sonne in hir awne handis, quhome sche left at Halyrudhous, accū-paneit w^t the Hamiltounis and sic vtheris as buir hir huisband na favo^r. In the mentyme ye erll Bothuell according to ye (6) devys appoynted betuix yame preparit for ye King y^t lugeine quhair he endit his lyif[15]. In quhat place it stuid, anew knawis and anew thoucht evin then y^t it ves ane rowine (ruin) vn-ganand to haif lugit ane prince in to, standing in a solitar place at the out moist p̄t of ye towne, separat frome all cumpanie, ane vaist rwynous hous quhairin na man haid dwelt sevin zeiris of befoir and finalie in all cōditiounis vnproper to haif placit ony honest mā vnto, y^t men of meanest jugemēt m^t haif jugit he wes no^t led y^r for ony vther purpois but as ane Lambe to ye slauchter as it succedit in deid. For it come navthervayis nor mē thoucht, seing ye circumstācis of hir strange and vnnaturall vsage of hym of befoir, hir, then to begyne to tak ane cair of his health y^t befoir (as we haif vreittin) sair handillit hyme. Howbeit na thingis ver left vndone y^t possible wer apperant to fyle (deceive) ye warld, said sche y^t it wes no^t for guid ayr (*sic*, probably should read— said she not, etc.) y^t he wes Luggit at ye Kirk of Feild how-beit in Scotland at ye begynnyng of Februar ane seik mā will content alsweill w^t ane clois and varme chalmer as ony air in ye feildis. Lay sche no^t in ye hous vnder hym in ye Thurisday and Fryday befoir he wes murthurit to gar ye pepill vnder-stand y^t sche wes begonne to Intertenye hym, and glaid sche wald haif bene y^t he my^t haif bene cuttit affe be ye p̄ticuleir querrell of sum vther, rathar nor be that meane of ye pulder y^t wes devysit[15]; for one ye Fryday sche tuik ye King, schaw-and hym of sum thingis qlk suld haif bene spokyn betuix hym and my Lord of Halyrudhous hir bruther qlk quhen he denyt, vpoun ye Setterday at afternowne, sche confronted yame togidder and never left to provock ye ane agains ye vther qll in hir awne presence sche causet yame fra vordis offer straikis to vther, and in hir p̅t it stuid no͏ᵗ bot yᵗ thai haid maid end of it yair, for sche wes no͏ᵗ cairfull quha suld be victor. Sche cryet on my Lord now Regent at ye same tyme and wald faine he suld haif bene p̅tiner wᵗ yat bargane[16] and abuif all studeit to haif hym p̅ñt in ye towne quhane yᵗ vnvorthie crueltie suld be cõmitted and purpoislie sent for hym to yᵗ effect, at ye cũing de Mossʳ du Moret, ye duik of Savoyis embassadour, quhair my Lord Regent remanit, qll vpoun Sunday ye ix day of Februar yᵗ passing to ye sermoune he ressauit ane lre purporting his vyif to be p̅ted wᵗ cheild and in extreme parrell of hir lyif, quhairwyᵗ being mowit he passit to ye Quene desyrand licence to dep̅t and veset hir, to quhome sche ansuerit yᵗ gif his wyif wes in sic perrell he neidit no͏ᵗ to pas for (7) his trawaill wald help hir nathing. Alwayis quhane he wrget to haif leif sche desyrit hym onlie to tarie yᵗ ane nyᵗ and he suld dep̅t in ye morne, bot of his away passing at yᵗ tyme God wes the authour and conducted hym, for haid he remanit yᵗ nyᵗ he haid taistet of yᵗ same coupe wᵗ the King, or thene suld haif bene subiect to ye sclander of ye varld as art and p̅t of yᵗ murthour. Qlk no͏ᵗwᵗstanding his absence thai burdeynit hym wᵗ be placardes affixit be ye erll of Huntlie and Bothuell. And vther vnleifull meanis for yair awne purgatioun bot ye trewthe can no͏ᵗ be smorit (smothered) nor horrible murthour concellit.

The tyme approching of ye executioun of yis wnnaturall crueltie, quhen na vther practize culd tak place, fering delay of tyme to oppin the cõspyrit purpois[17] ye Quene past vpoun ye Sunday after nowne, and after supper tyme, to ye hous quhair ye King wes luidgit and left na guid intertenemẽt wnschawin hym yᵗ sche culd wse passand ye tym mair familiarlie nor yᵗ ony vther tyme ye haill half zeir effoir, qll Pareis franchemã come in, quhome sa sonne as sche saw sche knew yᵗ the pulder wes put in the laiche hous wnder ye Kingis bed, for Pareis haid ye keyis baith of ye foir and bak dureis of yᵗ hous, and ye Kingis servandis haid ye haill remanent keyis of ye ludgene[18]; and sua rysand dissimulatlie sche said,—I haif faillit to Bastiane y^t hes no^t geven hym ye mask yis ny^t of his mariage, for qlk purpois I will pas to ye Abbay,—and sua dep̃tet w^t the erlis of Huntlie, Argyll and Cassillis. Y^t ny^t sche spak w^t ye erll Bothuell qll after xii houris and ye Lard of Tracquair being ye last man y^t wes w^{t}in ye house, saiffing he, left yame togidder, fra quhome quhene ye erll Bothuell dep̃tit, he past to his chalmer and yair changit his hois and dowblat and tuik his syde clok about hym and past vpe to ye accũplishment of y^t maist horrible murthour.

Ye forme and maner is veill aneuch declarit be yame y^t for ye same caus sufferit ye death. Sche, after ye erlis dep̃ting fra hir, never sleiptit qll ye crak, nor at ye noyis y^{r}of neuer mowit (for sche neidit no^t, vnderstanding ye purpois as sche did) qll ye erll Bothuell aros out of his bed and, accumpaneit w^t ye erlis Huntlie, Argyll, Atholl, ye countes of Atholl, Mar and ye Secretar, cũing to hir declarit how ye Kingis luggeine wes rasit and blawin in ye air and hym self ded, w^t qlk newis hir passiounis wes no^t sa gret nor hir cheare sa (8) havie as one in hir stait aucht to haif beine howbeit he haid no^t beine hir huisband bot ane comõun mã, for ye vnvorthines and strange exẽple (example) of ye deid. Sche derectet ye maist p̃t of yame to cõsidder ye maner w^t ye men of weir y^t wer in ye wacht. After qlk sche tuik rest w^t na sorifoull countenance for ony thing occurrit, qll neir at tuelfe howris at nowne one ye Mũunday; the hous in deid wes clois and ye ceremonye of ye dule obserwit howbeit wy^t schort space. For all mẽ in y^r hartis gruidgit to sie God sa mokkit be his creato^{rs}, and aeselie cõiecturit trewlie in ye trewthe. Naythar sche nor na vther meint to tak as samekill as ane forme of tryell and inquisitioun of sa odius a cryme then recentlie done, bot one ye Mũunday afternown ye cheif murtherar and vtheris cõvenit in ye erll of Argyllis luidgene begouth to spek of ye accident fallin, and as thai haid bene ignorãt yairof begouth to examinat sum wyiffis y^t haid spokyne rakleslie as thai thoucht bot no^t w^{t}out purpois. Quhairw^t being prickit thai desistit fra ony proceding in y^t examinatioun, fering ye furder thai diptet in it to fynd ye

gretar p̄rell thai left of and never wald spend ane houris trawaill in yᵗ behaulf¹⁹, bot promulgat a wane (vain) proclamatioun offerand to ony yᵗ wald reweill ye Kingis murthere riche
reward. But quha durst say yᵗ the Quene causit hir laufull
huisband to be murthurit or quha durst oppinlie affirme yᵗ ye
erll Bothuele yᵗ rewlit all wes ye authoʳ and executoʳ of sic
ane vnvorthe beaslie (beastly?) crueltie. Zeit thai restit noᵗ
lang vntheuchit (?) bot sic as outwartlie myᵗ noᵗ awoy (avow)
the threuth desistit not in syndrie vayis to lat ye varld vnder-
stand quhat a cloke mask wis wsit to cover sa vicket a cryme.
For tryell of ye placardeis prevelie set wp in accusatioun of ye
erlle Bothuell yʳ wes na paynis left nor hors flesche sparit. Yair
wes na payntoʳ to be found bot behuvit to gif his jugemĕt one
yᵗ qlk wes affixit vpoun ye Tolbwith duir of Edinburghe, and
almaist ane innocent mã haid sufferit gif God haid noᵗ mowit
ye virker (worker?) of ye thing to manifest hym self for releif
of ye vther. Schortlie on ye suddane ye tryell yᵗ aucht to
haif beine tane for ye murther of ye King wes transfarrit
agains yame yᵗ prevelie accusit ye erll Bothuele as his murtherar, and yʳ culd be na rest qll he wer clengit. Nor ye Quene
culd noᵗ wᵗ honestie proceid in ye purpois of mariage wᵗ hym
qll he wer first aquyte. This alsua is to be noted how hir
hatrait to ye King and his freindis sa cŏtenewit (9) after his
death yᵗ sche disponit his hors, armoʳ and quhatsumeuer ellis
p̄tenit hym, to ye verie authoʳˢ of his murthoʳ and vtheris his
gretest vnfreindis as gif all haid fallin in escheit and gart ye
oppressit wassellis (vassals) and frie tennentis of ye erledome
of Levenox componne for ye wardis of yair landis wᵗout respect
of yʳ oft (?) hairschippis (heirships?) of befoir, or to ye murthoʳ
of hir fl (faithful?) huisband yʳ superioʳ or to hir sonne now our
soverane Lordis ryᵗ and enteres (interest).

Now it is meit to returne agane and a litle discours vpoun
hir dissemblit and craiftie wsage after ye murthour. Howbeit
na craft seruit to ye peplis satisfactioun for negleckiting ye
ceremonye vsit be princes after ye deceis of yʳ huisbandis and
freindis, to keipe ane clois hous fourtie dayis wᵗout day lyᵗ.

Sche begouth the forme bot having ane vther thing in hir heid, ordour alterit and the circumstances of tyme wes no^t regardit, for four ny^{tis} wes no^t past quhen sche wereit of y^t counterfetit dule. Ye dure being closit sche culd fynd weile aneuche in hir hart, for all hir sorow, to luik to ye sonne and sie day ly^t w^{t}out hartbrek, and in speciell ane day maister Harie Killigrewe derectit in yis cuntrie be ye Quenis maiestie of England being sent for to cum to ye Quenis presence in ye palace of Haly-rudhous, howbeit he wes no^t suddane nor vndiscreit in his cũing, as he passit in ye hous ye vyndois wer oppin ye candillis scantlie ly^{c}tit and all thingis y^t suld haif beine in ordour befoir his cũing, disorderit^{20}. He my^t sie and p̄saue how hard it is to wse ypocrasie quhair God will haif it dis-closit. Of ye xl dayis dule sche culd no^t tarie at Halyrudhous abuif x or xii dayis and y^t w^t greit difficultie being in maist gret haard cais how to cõtrafeict dur (sic, dule?) and na thing les in hir mynd. Bot standing one na triflis sche come to ye lycht schortlie and past to Setoun having y^t place appoyntet as sche thoucht guid to hir towrne (turn) sum but no^t mony wer w^t hir, the erle Bothuell in speciell and howbeit hir credyt y^r in court, yea his awne place and rowme crawit hym to haif bene luidgit nixt hir self w^t the best, zeit his ludgeine wes wthervayis preparit. For evin beneth hir chalmer he wes placit in a hous joynit to ye kiching, it haid indeid a secreit turnepyk to hir chalmer, devysit to c̃woy meit prevelie frome ye kiching to ye chalmer gif neid requyrit, bot befoir y^t tyme neir ane in ye estait of ane nobilmã wes in y^t hous placit in sic a rowme, being a chalmer (howbeit proper aneuche) zeit mair meit for ye maister cuik in respect of ye situatioun nor for ony nobilmã, yair being sa mony comõdius places besydis to haif luidgit in qlk wer not occupeit be ony y^r, and gif thai wer, it wes be (10) sic as at ye moving of ye erll Bothuellis ee (eye) at that tyme wald haif gevin hym place. Bot ye turnepyk serwyt for y^r intentioun and vngodlie vsage. Monsr du Crokis cũing frome France causit yame schortlie cum agane to Edinbur^t, but ye place of Seytoun wes sa feit for y^t thing quhair in thai delytit that thai culd no^t tarie out of it bot schortlie returnit to it agane[21].

The counsele wes y^r cŏvenit in deid bot quhat wes yair consultatioun or quhairvpoun concludit thai that a day suld be set to clenge ye erll of Bothuell of ye Kingis murthour, becaus in ye placardis affixit and als be my Lord of Levenox lettres he wes delaitit as autho^r y^rof. The p̃liamĕt approchit at ye xiiii day of Aprile and befoir y^t he behuiffyt to haif ane assis. The erle of Levenox and vtheris ye Kingis servandis wer sum̃ondit to p̃sew, bot tyme vald no^t spair xv dayis varning as ye proces of y^t corrupt and inordinat court beris and quha sum̃ondit our souverane Lord, ye murthurit Kingis sonne, to p̃sew his fatheris murthour, or quhat swte maid ye Quene for tryell of his death y^t wes his awne flesche.

It it (*sic*, is?) trew y^t God at y^t tyme p̃mittit hym to obteyne ane countrafactet clengeine but to quhat purpois acquite of a murthour done on ye ix day qlk in deid wes com̃ittit vpoun ye x day. Ye erll of Levenox haid bot xiiii dayis varning, the King our soverane, thene prince, wes no^t varnit to p̃sew his faderis murthour nor zeit his tuto^rs or administrato^rs naythar zeit ye Quene ye Kingis vyif nor ye Quenis aduocatis. The cryme wes tressoun and y^t, as he y^t is callit on a tressonable cryme, aucht to be sum̃ondit on xl dayis varning according to ye lawes and practit of Scotland. For gif he y^t is suspectit to be ane tratour and com̃ittar of trassoun will swit his awne purgatioun, or gif ye prince in his favo^r will appoynt ye princes adwocatis to p̃sew ye nŏiat (nominate?) tratour to ye effect he may be clengit, Godis law, manis law and ressoun wald y^t ye freindis of yame aganis quhome ye trassoun is com̃ittit suld haif ye lyik favo^r and previlege of ye Law, and ye lyk space of xl dayis to p̃sew ye trato^r seking his awne purgatiŏ [or gif ye prince in his favo^r] as he suld haif haid in caice he haid beine callit at y^r instance and no^tw^tstanding all y^r suddane proceding at ye corrupt clengeine. And howbeit nane comperit derectlie to p̃sew zeit it may appeir got p̃at (*sic*, God put?) in ye hartis of y^t assis quhan a maist nakyt and symple protestatioun maid be a gẽtilman, servand of ye erll of Levenox (11) causit ye maist p̃t of ye p̃sounis of inqueist protest that thai suld incur ma (*sic*, na?) error becaus thai clengit in respect yᵗ nane comperit to sweir ye dittay as als thai clengit as ye same wes libellit yᵗ wes ane murthour cõmitted on ye ix day howbeit ye same wes murthurit vpoun ye x day. After this a cartell wes red and put one ye Mercat Croce of Edinburᵗ as a sup̃abundance aboue ye decreit of ye Law, offerand yᵗ noᵗwᵗstanding he wes acquyte zeit in forthir declaratioun of his innocencie he wald feicht wᵗ ony erle, lord barroun or gentilmã vndefamit yᵗ wald allege hym authour of the Kingis murthour and thai vantit noᵗ xxiiii houris ansʳ althoucht noᵗ awowit then, bot wᵗin litill mair nor a moneth he vanted noᵗ ansʳ in derect termes as is veilaneuch knawin to all men²².

Quhen ye clengeine wes done yʳ wes thoucht na forther to hauld bak ye intentit conclusioun onlie vii or viii dayis wer spent in ye p̃liamẽt for ye erll of Huntlieis restitutioun, howbeit vther thingis wer in heid. To pacifie stormes and eschew gretar evill wᵗ litill difficultie, actis wer past in favoʳ of ye trew religioun and all penall Lawes maid in ye contrare in tyme of papistrie abolishit. Bot zeit it culd noᵗ be wᵗout sclandʳ yᵗ the Quene suld gang oppinlie to bed wᵗ the erll Bothuele yᵗ haid a mareit vyif of his awne. Howbeit of befoir and then, thai sparit na tyme to fulfill yʳ vngodlie appetit, zeit sum quhat to covere hir honestie sche behuwit to be reuest, qlk wes broucht to pas schortlie yʳefter as sche returnit frome Stirveling to Edinburᵗ and quhether yᵗ proceidit of hir self or noᵗ hir letter vreittin to ye erll Bothuell out of Lynlytquo can declair. Being còwoyit be hym to Dumbar in continent thai causet a diuorcie be mowyt in dowble forme agains his laufull vyif, befoir ye ordinar cõmissaris establischit be ye Kingis authoritie and als befoir sum jugeis delegate, constitute be ye beshope of Sanctãdr̃s, as gif ye Papis vsurpit autõ (authority) zeit haid place in yis realme. The first, p̃sewit be a procuratorie of his laufull vyif ye erll of Huntleis sister (qlk sche wes compellit to mak) for adulterie cõmittit on his p̃t befoir, ye vtheris, for causes of

consanguinitie, abstractand ye dispensatioun, bot yʳ wes noᵗ
delay in nather of ye jugemẽts, aucht or x ten (*sic*) dayis endit
baith ye process. Sche cõtenewing to ye eyis of ye warld and
as hir self wald seame captiwe all this tyme in Dumbar, bot
howsoune newis come of thir sẽtences of diuorce pronõcit, his
freindis in ye Mers and all the boundis of Eist Lowthiane being
send for wer cõvenit to cõwoye ye Quene to Edinburᵗ in veir
lyk maner, qlk in yʳ passagis enterit in questioun yᵗ sum day
it myᵗ be said ye Quene wes captiue and cõvoyit (12) as pre-
sonar in veirlykmaner and that thai myᵗ be accusit yairefter
of ye same, yairfor in ye mydway thai laid yair speris fra thame
and sua cõwoyit hir to Edinburᵗ Castell, quhair sche remanit
certane dayis wnto ye proclamatioun of hir bannis and then
sche past to the Tolbuith and in presence of ye Lordis of Counsell declarit sche wes at libertie, and sua wᵗin aucht dayis passit
to the cõsumatioun of that vngodlie mariage yᵗ all ye warld
comptes nawchtie and a mokking of God. The tyme wes noᵗ
long betuix ye same pretendit mariage qlk wes maid one ye
xv day of Maii 1567 and the xv day of Junii yairefter, yᵗ after
ye said erlis fleing, sche come to ye Lordis²³ assemblit for re-
venge of ye murtheur, and zeit in yᵗ monithis space quhat con-
fusioun and corruptioun wes yair to behauld it wes mervelous.
All nobilmen for ye maist p̃t wᵗ drew yame, and sic as tareit
how affectionat yᵗ euer that euer (*sic*) thai schew yame selfis
to Hʳ m (Her Majesty?) zeit wer thai in na better grace nor
ye vtheris yᵗ vtterlie gaif our (over) ye court, as ye Q(uenis)
billis frome Glescow to ye erlle Bothuele and at mony vther
tymes declaris²⁴.

(*The matter here following is additional to that of the Latin
"Detection," but the style is so similar that it is further evidence
that the document under consideration is by Buchanan.*)

It is noᵗ heir to be neglectit or past over wyᵗ silence³ quhat
danger ye Innocent p̃soun of ye King, now our soverane, stud
yair in, quhen befoir ye murtheur of his fader he wes careit in
ye cauld vynter as we haif befoir said fra Stirveling to Halyrudhous, nor how after ye murtheur, after he wes ains devisat

to be send agane to Stirveling the purpois stayit and ye pro-
ponaris wer estemit na guid freindis to ye Quene, qll Edinburᵗ
Castell wes to be rainderit furth of ye erle of Maris handis to
fordir qlk purpois he wes transported in deid to Stirveling, qlk
wes noᵗ sa sone done bot assone it wes repentit yᵗ euer he suld
haif past out of yʳ handis. And no doubt ye Quene (*sic*) maist
principall erand of ane wes to bring hym away quhene sche
past to Stirveling after ye p̃liamēt and befoir hir revesing, and
zeit gold (*sic*, God?) wald noᵗ p̃mit it. Yair wes ane army or-
danit to be cōvenit agane ye said xv day of Junii as to haif
past one the thewis (thieves), bot sic as wer prewye knew weill
aneuche and ye com̃oun pepill sparit noᵗ at yᵗ same tyme to
spek yᵗ it wes to bring ye King furth of Stirling agane, qll ye
Quene, to satisfye ye pepill set out a proclamatioun declaring
na sic thing to be in hir heid. For sche cōsiderit the gruydge
remaning in ye hartis of hir subiectis qlk cōtinuallie murmurit
yᵗ the innocent orphaine wald be send after his father gif euer
he come in ye handis of yame yᵗ murthurit hym, sua feir to
offend ye pepill at yᵗ tym be Godis m̃cifull providence stayit
ye purpois of ye princis transporting vnto sic sic (*bis*) tyme as
God mowit vther materis for yame to think of²⁵.

Now lat hir cōtenewit hetrent and disdane agains ye King hir
laufull huisband be considerit quhow sche sterit vpe and inter-
teneit hatrent and dissentioun betuix hym and ye nobilitie and
causit his servandis quhome sche appoyntet to await vpoun hym
of befoir to leif hym. How his plat and weschell wer takyne
fra hym and he miserabilie (13) left lyand in Glescow destitute
of all guid confort and intertenemēt. And one ye vther p̃t,
let, first ye familiaritie betuix ye Quene and ye erll Bothuell
be considerit, and fra yᵗ how neglectand God and honestie
thai cōtenewit in fylthie adulterie as cleirlie apperis.............
send to hym, qll betuix yame thai haid compass.................
put in executioun ye death and destructioun of.................
franschemā quhome befoir ony vther thai vs......................
tyme can veill declair, he is p̃ntlie in Denmark.................
wer ye Quenis Maiestie of Englandis guid p....................

he wer habill to resolue mony thingis in yis.......................
vther in ye varld besydis yame y^t vsit.............................
sequele following prewis all y^t precedit ye.......................
for lamentatioun sche maid nane. Inquisitioun and tryall of
ye murth..
was neglectit. Hir blind raige and inordinat affectioun vald
no^t suffer hir to contrafete dule. Gret pane sche tuik in deid
to haif knawlege of yame y^t bruitet and accusit ye said erle
as authour of ye murtheur, sche neuer restit qll sche haid
hym clengit as is befoir said, hir self for a fassioun revist,
diuorce betuix hym and his laufull vyif led, and in cõclusioun
ye Quene and he cupplit togidder in y^t vnlaufull and pretendit
mariage. Quairby, as alsua be hir awne handvreit in mony and
syndrie letteris send betuix yame during ye cours of y^t vickyt
tyme, it is maist patent, trew and euident y^t sche wes no^t onlie
previe of ye same horrible and vnnaturall murtheur but als ye
verray instrumẽt, cheif organe and principall causer of y^t vnnaturall crueltie, p̃petrat in ye p̃soun of hym y^t wes hir laufull
huisband and be Godis law ane flesche w^t hir self, befoir ye
cõmitting quhairof (as planlie apperis) sche no^t onlie be vords
bot be vreiting promist to tak ye erle Bothuele to [vyif]
huisband, quhairin, albeit for a colo^r sche disdanfullie termes
ye King, vmqll Henrie Stewart of Darlie hir lait huisband, zeit
it apperis veill becaus ye lre (letter) is w^{t}out a deit y^t it hes
bene vreittin and subscriuit befoir ye murther for on ye v day
of Aprill y^{r}efter no^{t}w^{t}standing ye mariage standing betuix hym
and his vyif, sche enterit in a plane and a new cõtract w^t hym
as ye samyn vreittin be ye erll of Huntlie and subscriuit w^t
baith y^r handis proportis, sua y^t y^r laikis na pruife and testifie
a multitude of infallible presumptiounis.

NOTES ON THE TEXT OF THE MANUSCRIPT

PAGE 1 There are a number of erasures, repetitions and cases of overrunning by the copyist, as also cases wherein the English orthography has been used, presumably in error. The document is certainly a copy, probably hastily written by an English clerk from a Scottish original.

33 2 The return from Dunbar was after the murder of Rizzio, but this subject is avoided in all the documents dealing with the Queen's concern in the death of her husband.

34, 47 3 The expression, 'It is not to be passed over in silence,' is used twice in the manuscript before us. It also occurs in the *Admonition to the Trew Lordis*, an undoubted Buchanan writing. It may have been a common phrase, but I have not found it elsewhere in the documents connected with the case, and it seems to be some additional proof that Buchanan was the author.

35 4 The use of the word 'becrasit' may be intentional, but it may be an error for 'betrayed,' the word used in the *Detection*.

35 5 The Latin word is 'zona' which Wilson translates as 'string,' Buchanan puts it more correctly as 'belt.' The Hopetoun MS omits this part of the story.

35 6 The use of the word, 'commission,' has a certain interest; here it means the mandate given by the Queen. In the old French the word was usually applied to the command of a prince, and this has a bearing on the interpretation of the words in the 'short' Glasgow Letter: "According to my Commission etc.," which is always held to mean, 'according to the instructions received from you (Bothwell) I will do so and so,' whereas it means, 'according to the orders or arrangements I (Mary) have given or made I will do so and so.'

35 7 There is a special interest attaching to this clause. It is well known that Dalgleish's Deposition contains no such reference. Malcolm Laing, whose zeal to accumulate matter against the Queen outran his discretion, was troubled by the omission. It was an evidence that the Deposition had been doctored! He therefore explained that the words in the original Latin: "Quae ejus confessio in actis continetur," are an interpolation made by Wilson when translating the paper in 1571. (See Laing, *Hist. of Scotland*, II. p. 4, *et seq.*). *In actis*, says Laing, refers to the *Journal of the Commission* at Westminster, *Confessio* refers to the Confession and not to the judicial deposition recorded in the Books of the Scottish Privy Council. In our paper, however, we have enough to demolish Laing's argument. In what we believe to be Buchanan's own words, written long before the Westminster Commission, the existence of the clause in the original Latin is confirmed and *Confessio* is rendered Deposition.

36   8 The Earl of Moray, himself, was one of the company, hence we find this statement is toned down in the Hopetoun *Book of Articles* to the danger from thieves on the road. It is a small evidence of the priority of our paper.

36   9 The original was probably, 'day and night.'

37   10 This long story of Darnley's assiduity to visit his sick wife does not accord with contemporary opinion.

37   11 The contents of this letter are not on record. Probably it was connected with the delicate negotiations then proceeding for a Papal subsidy. John Beton had brought the first instalment in the previous September, but further supply was only to be made on conditions inimical to the protestant notabilities which Mary refused to agree to. A 'gentleman' of the Cardinal of Lorraine had been despatched with very secret letters to persuade her, who would have arrived at (probably) Leith early in November, while the Queen was still at Jedburgh; it seems likely that Darnley had obtained knowledge of the affair. He had already taken some steps to cross the Queen's purpose (*Simancas*, I. 507) and this letter of his was doubtless a continuance of his action. Buchanan refers to the Cardinal's letter in his *History* and declares that Mary communicated it to Moray. The incident is interesting but cannot be fully dealt with here; much information is obtainable from the correspondence in Father Pollen's *Papal Negotiations*.

37   12 It is here suggested that the idea of divorce originated from the Queen, but this is contrary to other and more reliable statements.

38   13 Pansit = thought over, is a gallicism reminiscent of Buchanan. There are several others in the document.

39   14 The festivities of the baptism ended on the 23rd December. The Earl of Morton's pardon must have been granted about this date. Probably Darnley fled from Stirling as soon as this was decided. It had evidently been the intention for Bothwell to accompany the Earl of Bedford, the Queen was anxious to do him (Bedford) as much honour as possible. I think the retention of Bothwell and no doubt also the Secretary, Lethington, was on account of the complication brought about by Darnley's escapade. The houses of Drymen (Drummond Castle) and Tullibardine lay about 16 and 12 miles respectively north of Stirling. It is worth noting, though perhaps there is little in it, that the register of Privy Seal Deeds indicates that the Queen returned to Stirling on 30th December after the visit to Drymen, also that she was at Tullibardine on the 31st. It is strange that she should pass the latter place and return to it again. The Lennox-Cecil journal says that she returned to Stirling on the 31st, but this is doubtful. Apparently Bothwell left Stirling before the 2nd January for he was not at the Privy Council held at Stirling on that date, I think it likely that he had been sent to Dunbar to open negotiations with Morton as to the terms of his pardon. There remains the possibility that Drymen does

not in fact mean 'The Lord Drummondis Hous' (as stated in the Hopetoun Paper and the Lennox Journal, both suspect documents), but the town of that name. If Darnley were making for the Clyde when he left Stirling, it is not unlikely that he would go by Drymen and Dumbarton. Did Mary follow him and return as soon as she learnt of his having gone to Glasgow and of his illness? Let us recall the words in the alleged letter from Glasgow, to Bothwell, "Sr James Hamiltoun met me quha schew yat ye vyer tyme quhen he (Lennox) hard (heard) of my cuming, he departit away etc." When was 'The other time'?

40   15 These two references to the previous preparation of the house in Edinburgh are out of accord with the 'evidence' of the *Casket Letters*; it seems unlikely that the final edition of the *Book of Articles* (of which there is no copy) contained them in this form.

41   16 This reference to Moray's knowledge of the case is suppressed in the Hopetoun MS.

41   17 The first Lennox narrative gives what is probably the true reason why the Sunday night was chosen for the explosion, viz. that Darnley was to have returned to Holyrood the following day.

41   18 The statements as to possession of the Keys vary in all the narratives.

43   19 Whatever was done or left undone to discover the plot that ended Darnley's life, it can hardly be said that the Queen was responsible. There can be little doubt that she was reduced to a state not far from collapse. Innocent or guilty she was not the kind of woman who could undergo such an experience unmoved. Her medical life history is a guarantee of this and does not need the corroboration that the Council and doctors insisted on removing her from the scene and put an end to the somewhat barbarous 'period of dule.' In any case the Earl of Moray was recalled and was in Edinburgh early in March. It does not appear that he had any better success than the others.

44   20 This part of the story seems curiously disordered. Killigrew arrived in Edinburgh on the 19th or 20th February but did not see the Queen until 8th March. He was the bearer of important letters, one an autograph from Elizabeth, connected with the successful negotiations carried out by Bedford at the time of the baptism. Mary had high hopes from this and undoubtedly would not have deferred audience for some 16 days if she had been able to avoid it. The whole story is misleading, for Mary had been taken to Seton before Killigrew arrived, on the 16th or 17th of February, and remained there until at least the 3rd March; probably on her return she was still too ill to see Killigrew until the 8th. At the end of March, Drury wrote to Cecil that she was still ill and she apparently returned to Seton about the 28th or 29th and remained to, perhaps, the 10th April as stated in the Lennox-Cecil Journal.

45 21 Again the story is misleading. De Croc could not have reached Edinburgh before the 3rd of April. His presence had obviously no connection with the Queen's movements, see preceding note. The careless inaccuracy of these statements which could most easily have been checked at the time shows pretty clearly that Moray's Party at Westminster relied on the partial character of the enquiry.

46 22 This somewhat confused paragraph departs considerably from the Latin and is much shortened and simplified in the Hopetoun MS, yet the general similarity of the idea can be followed in both. Buchanan in his history follows the Latin very closely.

47 23 The free rendering of the Latin paper, *De Maria etc.*, ends at this point, all that follows is matter which must be considered as afterthoughts of Buchanan tending to add to the effect of the first hasty compilation. It is interesting to compare this with the later works of the Hopetoun MS and the *History*. The dates given in the Latin are now corrected.

47 24 It can hardly be said that either of the *Glasgow Letters* indicates this.

48 25 This paragraph bears several indications of the authorship of Buchanan. The opening line has been referred to at note (3) above. The story of removing the Earl of Mar from the command of Edinburgh castle in exchange for the custody of the Prince, is told in somewhat similar fashion in the *History*, which was completed from Buchanan's notes, though probably not by himself. I do not know of its appearing elsewhere. Similarly the idea of the Queen's desire to recover the person of the Prince is mentioned in both as the reason for her visit to Stirling in April. There is also indistinct allusion to the operations at Borthwick as being connected, on the part of the Lords, with the defence of the 'Innocent Person' of the prince. No reference is made in the *History* or in the Hopetoun MS to the Proclamation referred to. It was issued on June 1st at Edinburgh and a copy is printed by Keith (vol. II. p. 612). Mar had been appointed as custodian of the child in the previous October when the Queen went to Jedburgh, he was in fact, in a sense, the hereditary guardian. His father had acted in the same capacity to Mary herself and to her father. Writing to Mar in December 1568, from her prison at Bolton, she said, "I gave you both the one and the other (that is her son and charge of Stirling Castle) because of the faith I had in you and yours," she added, "Remember that when I gave in your charge my son as my most precious treasure, you promised to guard him and not to deliver him without my consent." It is in the plots which centre round the possession of the baby prince that the true explanation of the tragedy of Mary Stuart will probably be found.

The last paragraph is a peroration which Buchanan would not be likely to omit. The Record has been damaged and unfortunately the part lost contains a reference to the Frenchman 'Paris' which might be interesting. It appears to suggest that if it were the Queen of England's good pleasure to procure the person of 'Paris,' at that time in Denmark, much evidence would result. Now in fact, 'Paris' was handed over to one Clark, a captain in the Danish service, in the latter end of October. This enables us to confirm the date of our Paper as prior to this event. However, 'Paris' was not apparently wanted by those who controlled the affair and he was not brought to Scotland until the following year. 'Paris,' when examined—in the presence of Buchanan—*was*, "hable to resolue mony thingis," but what he had to say was carefully and very suspiciously suppressed, and nobody could read his story without a doubt that it was freely embroidered by the inquisitors. If Buchanan believed in it, it is remarkable that he neither used it nor mentioned it in his *History*.

These notes deal only with points relevant to a consideration of the Cambridge Manuscript. Many other statements in it and in the parallel *Detection* are disputable and are dealt with by other writers.

Printed in the United States
by Bookmasters

Printed in the United States
By Bookmasters